MINORITIES IN AMERICAN LIFE
THE IRISH IN THE UNITED STATES

JOHN B. DUFF

THE IRISH IN
THE UNITED STATES

MINORITIES IN AMERICAN LIFE SERIES

General Editor: Alexander DeConde
University of California, Santa Barbara

THE IRISH IN THE UNITED STATES, John B. Duff, Seton Hall University

THE CHALLENGE OF THE AMERICAN DREAM: THE CHINESE IN THE UNITED STATES, Francis L. K. Hsu, Northwestern University

FORTHCOMING

THE SOCIETY AND CULTURE OF THE MEXICAN AMERICANS, Jesus Chavarria, University of California, Santa Barbara

THE AMERICAN POLES, Louis L. Gerson, University of Connecticut

BLACK URBAN AMERICA SINCE RECONSTRUCTION, Hollis R. Lynch, Columbia University

THE JAPANESE AMERICAN, Setsuko M. Nishi, Brooklyn College

JEWISH CULTURE IN THE UNITED STATES IN THE 20TH CENTURY, Milton Plesur, State University of New York at Buffalo

ITALIAN CULTURE AND HISTORY IN THE UNITED STATES, Andrew F. Rolle, Occidental College

THE NEGRO CULTURE IN THE SOUTH SINCE THE CIVIL WAR, Arnold H. Taylor, University of Connecticut

THE IRISH IN
THE UNITED STATES

JOHN B. DUFF
SETON HALL UNIVERSITY

WADSWORTH PUBLISHING COMPANY, INC., BELMONT, CALIFORNIA

For Mary Cunningham Duff
My Mother · One Who Came
from Ireland to America

L. C. Cat. Card No.:
70–149014
ISBN–0–534–00038–X

Printed in the United States of
America

1 2 3 4 5 6 7 8 9 10—
75 74 73 72 71

SERIES PREFACE

The *Minorities in American Life* series is designed to illuminate hitherto-neglected areas of America's cultural diversity. Each author treats problems, areas, groups, or issues that cannot ordinarily be examined in depth in the usual surveys of American history and related subjects. Although all the volumes are connected to each other through the unifying theme of minority cultures, the series is flexible and open to a number of uses. For example, two or more volumes can be used as units in a comparative study. Each will bring out the distinctive features of an ethnic group, but together the books may show the common as well as the unique features and experiences of each minority studied.

In varying degrees every book includes narrative, analysis, and interpretation. Each is written simply, clearly, and intelligently by an authority on its subject, and all reflect the most recent scholarship. Some restate, with fresh insights, what scholars may already know; others present new syntheses, little-known data, or original ideas related to old concepts; and all are intended to stimulate thought, not merely to pass on information. By opening minority studies to young people, the series also meets a social and educational need. By providing short, sound, and readable books on their life and culture, and by accepting them on their own terms, the series accords minorities the justice and appreciation for their heritage that they have seldom received. By dealing with live issues in a historical context, it also makes the role of minority culture in American life meaningful to young people and opens new doors to an understanding of the American past and present.

Alexander DeConde

ACKNOWLEDGMENT

Any author owes a large debt to those who counseled and encouraged him. I particularly want to acknowledge the help I received from Peter M. Mitchell, my colleague in the History Department of Seton Hall University, who read and improved the manuscript, suggesting several sensible changes and additions. Thomas A. Duff eliminated many lapses in style and grammar with his blue pencil. I am grateful to Misses Ana Alves, Eileen O'Neil, and Maryanne Sobowicz, each of whom typed portions of the book. As has been true in every aspect of my life for the past fifteen years, my largest debt I owe to my wife Helen.

CONTENTS

Chapter One

Introduction

The Irish have been a special source of interest in minority group studies because, in spite of the rigors of the process, they have successfully blended into the American mainstream. On January 20, 1961, John Fitzgerald Kennedy, the grandson of an immigrant, took the "same solemn oath" that Washington had sworn nearly two centuries earlier. Kennedy's inaugural was, in one sense, a symbolic tribute to the Irish who came to America.

This book is an assessment of their contribution to American life. It attempts to give the reader an understanding of the Irish through a discussion of a variety of topics: their hatred of the English, their earliest American settlements, the widespread immigrations to this country caused by the potato famine of the nineteenth century, their struggles to win and keep employment, their canny political skill and reliance upon democratic processes to change their lives, their proud and continuous love of their homeland, their Roman Catholic religion, its strength and influence.

In Shakespeare's history play *King Henry IV Part II* the monarch advises his son Prince Hal "to busy giddy minds with foreign quarrels," and English kings until the twentieth century had busied themselves and their subjects in a running feud with Ireland, a most accessible island. The rule of Ireland by the English from the twelfth century on was reason enough to explain Irish hostility. But later, a second major cause arose: In the sixteenth century, Henry the Eighth broke with Rome, creating the (Protestant) Church of England. Most of the Irish remained Catholic, so new fuel was added to the fires of the English-Irish enmity. Irish colonial migration, always steady, grew to mass-exodus proportions because of the potato famine of the nineteenth century.

And a bleak life it was that welcomed the new immigrant. Row after row of shanty towns linked by circling smoke and rude clotheslines were the living conditions he could expect. If he were fortunate to escape the machinations of confidence men and "shanghai runners," he could hope to stake a claim in physical labor, occasionally escaping into the relief of a whiskey reverie to bolster his self-esteem and to help him forget his humble station.

He chose to fight it out in the dangerous city rather than turn to the West. The comradeship and community he had left in the old country were comforting, and he knew they could not be found in American farming. Like the races and nationalities which followed him, he lived in the ghetto tenements, committing the crimes and wreaking the violence that history has proved poverty and abominable conditions invariably breed.

The Irish catapulted from the obscurity of railroad laborers into the glory of military heroes because of their bravery on the battlefields of the American Civil War. Curiously, although they fought in overwhelming numbers for the Union cause, many Irish showed open hostility towards blacks before and after the war, because they considered them competitors in the labor marketplace—though the Irish themselves encountered the prejudice of nativist groups such as the Know-Nothing Party in the antebellum years and the American Protective Association at the turn of the century.

That old loyalties were not forgotten is shown in the Irish concern for the fate of their mother country. In nineteenth century America, the Fenians, a revolutionary group, and the writings of John Devoy helped to sustain interest in Ireland's future. Picnics and socials which brought the Irish together functioned as a means of discussing old grievances. In 1916, when Woodrow Wilson failed to protest England's suppression of the Irish Easter Week uprising, the Irish in America began to have doubts about the President's concern; and during the negotiations following the war, when Wilson became annoyed at the importuning of the members of the American Commission for Irish Independence and failed to do anything, the Irish felt they had been mistreated. In overwhelming numbers the Irish repudiated Wilson, and their opposition helped kill his hopes to have the United States join the League of Nations.

From the earliest years of their migration, the American Irish had been interested in politics and had developed the knowledge and skills to enable them to excel in the political art. Saloonkeepers had formed associations; firemen or policemen had banded together for social reforms; neighborhood politicos saw to it that new immigrants found work, or otherwise they gave real assistance to those in need. By the 1890s, most of the great cities of the nation had Irish political machines. In the twentieth century, Alfred E. Smith and John F. Kennedy both ran for the presidency; the distance between 1928 and 1960 in American thinking enabled Kennedy to win in spite of his religious beliefs.

Religion, of course, had always been a source of great solace for the Irish and a cause for fear among their American neighbors. Fantasy abetted by rumor preyed upon the imagination: Natives saw the Pope manipulating the strings under which danced a puppet Irish-Catholic President. Clearly, disputes arose within the Church over the political and social issues in American life, so that the labels liberal and conservative may be interchanged in reference to Irish clerical leaders in given situations at different points in American history. The Catholic Church in the United States, still primarily Irish in its hierarchical personnel at present, appears ready to fulfill the teaching of the Vatican II Council to become a more effective force in alleviating the social injustices of the modern world.

The Irish experience in America, then, is at once varied and valuable. By looking at the social, economic, political, religious, military, and cultural contributions, we may produce a good effect, one which all minority groups in America need most: *understanding.*

This book will mention many famous Irish-Americans, yet it should be said that, like most immigrants, those Irish who made the greatest sacrifices will remain unknown to the rest of mankind. The laborers, men and women, the countless nuns and priests who willingly gave up the world to serve as educators, social workers administering to the sick and aged, the long-forgotten ancestors whose names are heard rarely by their current descendants—to them the country owes more than what honor she has awarded to her most popular Irish offspring.

General Sources

Abbott, Edith, *Historical Aspects of the Immigration Problem: Select Documents,* Chicago, 1926.

Degler, Carl N., *Out of Our Past: The Forces That Shaped Modern America,* New York, 1959.

Glazer, Nathan, and Daniel P. Moynihan, *Beyond the Melting Pot: The Negroes, Puerto Ricans, Jews, Italians and Irish of New York City,* Cambridge, Mass., 1963.

Handlin, Oscar, *The Uprooted,* Boston, 1951.

Jones, Maldwyn, *American Immigration,* Chicago, 1960.

Shannon, William V., *The American Irish,* New York, 1963.

Wittke, Carl, *The Irish in America,* Baton Rouge, 1956.

————, *We Who Built America,* Revised Edition, Cleveland, 1964.

Chapter Two

Colonial Beginnings and the Great Migration

To what causes may we trace the traditional Irish dislike and distrust of England? It is a tale of political and religious differences not unlike the contrary views separating the present-day Irish in the North and South of their island. And it helps explain why, during the great famine, the Irish sailed not to England but to distant America. It was the lure of a two-fold blessing: to sail away from economic and political discrimination, to sail toward freedom and opportunity.

We should begin our story not in the United States but in the Ireland of centuries ago: Before there was an Irish-American there was an Irishman. As with no other immigrant people except the Jews, the heritage of their past deeply affected the Irish in America. They remembered the haunting beauty of the old country and its trying history. Ever since Richard Strongbow crossed the Irish Sea at the head of an invading English Army in 1170, it had been a time wounded by wars, insurrections, looting, destruction, death. In the sixteenth century, the English Reformation introduced a new element: religious persecution. The Irish, clinging to their old faith, found themselves subject to rigorous penal laws.

Accustomed to rebelling to preserve their Gaelic language and culture and the semblance of "semi-independent" Catholic Ireland, the Irish viewed their resistance to any attempt to extend Anglicanism in Ireland as a holy war. Catholic Celts made a determined effort to prevent English penetration beyond the Pale, the area around Dublin that the conquerors had controlled for centuries. The English undertook expansion into central and Northern Ireland, into the provinces of Munster, Connaught, and Ulster, to provide land for the indigent or rapacious members of the new Tudor gentry. Such penetration began in the time of Elizabeth the First, but the necessity of protecting acquired territories led the English, inevitably, to the conquest of the entire island. Irish resistance was prolonged and most nearly successful in Ulster, where the Earls of Tyrone and Tyrconnel, O'Neil and O'Donnell, provided timely leadership and the stuff of which heroic ballads are made. But they, too, suffered ultimate defeat and banishment, and the subjection continued.

Oliver Cromwell finished all resistance—or so he hoped—in 1649 with one of the most brutal and bloodthirsty military slaughters in history. Cromwell's destructiveness in Ireland once had its defenders, notably Thomas Carlyle, in the nineteenth century; but Winston Churchill, a more representative Englishman and incomparably finer historian, thought Cromwell's Irish campaign "a deed of frightfulness," "a massacre so all-effacing as to startle even the opinion of those fierce times." He wrote that Cromwell, "disposing of overwhelming strength and using it with merciless wickedness, debased the standards of human conduct and sensibly darkened the journey of mankind."

After ruthlessly crushing the rebellion, Cromwell then ordered a virtual proscription of the Catholic religion and imposed an iniquitous land settlement. His soldiers methodically dispossessed thousands from their holdings; men were given the choice of death or exile—"Hell or Halifax." Contractors of labor arrived from England to round up the able-bodied for work in remote colonies. In one typical instance, a Captain John Vernon, employed by the English commissioner in Ireland, contracted to find "two hundred and fifty women of the Irish nation above twelve years and under fifty . . . in the country within twenty miles of Cork, Youghal Consale, Waterford and Wexford, [and] to transport them into New England." In four years, 4400 were thus dispatched overseas. On this unhappy note began the Irish migration to America.

Before long, however, others were going of their own accord. Historians traditionally have summed up the motives for migration from Europe to the new world with the words *Glory, God,* and *Gold.* And did not the new world attract those of a restless nature seeking adventure and change? Beckon to the pious seeking a sanctuary for the unfettered practice of their religion? Provide an opportunity for the ambitious to achieve the good life of abundance and security? This last goal certainly came first with those Catholic Irish who came to America of their own volition before the American Revolution, although, admittedly, since most made their way to Maryland and Pennsylvania, where a greater tolerance of their faith prevailed, the religious motivation was not absent from their considerations.

Chiefly, however, they wanted to improve themselves, and were willing to emigrate as indentured servants or redemptioners. In exchange for passage to America they bound themselves to labor, customarily for a period of three to five years but sometimes as long as seven. At the end of the term of service, they were to be provided with clothes, money, and, occasionally, land. In addition to those who willingly signed articles of indentures, others found themselves kidnapped to America. Traffic in servants could be quite lucrative, and some English agents, or "spirits," gained an unsavory reputation for kidnapping. The victim, plied with liquor or knocked insensible, would be hurried aboard a darkling ship. One young Irishman testified in a Massachusetts court that he "with divers others were stolen in Ireland, by some of the English soldiers in the night out of their beds and brought to Mr. Dills ship where the boat lay ready to receive them."

Despite the earnest effort of colonial authorities to regulate treatment of indentured servants, their lot does not appear to have been an easy one. Some contemporaries believed their condition to be worse than that of Negro slaves. Yet, though considerable hostility and discrimination against the Irish beyond that shown other white indentured servants appears to have been commonplace, fear and hatred of the "turbulent and dangerous Irish" never persuaded white men to make them slaves, in any verifiable case.

As might be expected, a goodly number of those brought to the colonies against their will made off at the first chance. In certain areas, few of the runaways were ever recaptured. The *Maryland Gazette* for March 16, 1769, carried an advertisement for a fugitive servant, a poem inserted by a master with a wry sense of humor and a flair for verses, if not for verse:

> Last Wednesday noon at break of day
> From Philadelphia ran away,
> An Irishman named John McKeohn,
> To fraud and imposition prone;
> About five feet, five inches high,
> Can curse and swear as well as lie;
> How old he is I can't engage
> But forty-five is near his age. . . .
>
> He oft in conversation chatters
> Of scripture and religious matters,
> And fain would to the world impart,
> That virtue lodges in his heart;
> But take the rogue from stem to stern,
> The hypocrite you'll soon discern—
> And find (tho' his deportment's civil)
> A saint without, within a devil.
> Who'er secures said John McKeohn
> (Provided I can get my own),
> Shall have from me, in cash paid down,
> Five dollar bills, and half a crown.

Indentured servants have sometimes been portrayed as the founders of the first families of Virginia and Maryland. This tale is mostly fancy, but several indentures did overcome the limitations of their beginnings and go on to distinguished careers. Matthew Lyon emigrated from County Wicklow in 1765 as a servant; after his indenture he enjoyed a successful business career and served in Congress from Vermont and Kentucky. As a congressman he combatted antidemocratic tendencies in the early republic and led the opposition against the Alien and Sedition Acts.

The Irish population in America grew slowly in the second half of the eighteenth century. During the turbulent years of the French Revolution, just as the century ended, French-encouraged rebellion in Ireland followed by English repression caused emigration to rise again. Not until after the final defeat of Napoleon in 1815, however, did it become an ever-widening stream, hundreds swelling to thousands of people.

Why did they come? In these early years of the American Republic it was an article of democratic faith to regard the United States as a potent magnet, attracting all those seeking civil liberty and freedom of belief. Americans axiomatically believed that a longing for political and religious freedom was the chief motivation of the immigrants. Such beliefs may not be taken lightly. For many Irish the opportunity to escape hated English rule drew them west across the ocean.

But for most who emigrated before 1840, and for the great bulk who came after that date, the chance for a better life, or indeed survival itself, was the prime consideration. Some of the first to leave were substantial farmers attracted by the abundance of free land; as the nineteenth century advanced, others had no choice save to leave Ireland or sink into pauper status. For centuries, land had been the basis of existence; now holdings had shrunk progressively as generations of fathers attempted to provide for their sons by dividing the family's meagre holdings among all the male heirs.

Near 1780, for reasons that are not ascertainable even today, the population of the country had taken a sudden and prodigious leap upward. In the next 60 years the increase was a staggering 172 percent, creating a population of over eight millions, making Ireland the most densely populated country in Europe and creating absurdities of division and subdivision of land. In a large family a legacy of land is crucial to survival. When, for example, four sons survived to manhood, the problem of division was compounded. Each son received 75 percent less land than he might have, had he been the sole survivor.

By the 1840s over 560,000 of the 690,000 agricultural holdings in Ireland consisted of fewer than 15 acres. The difficulty of trying to eke out a comfortable living from such tiny plots was aggravated by an iniquitous land system controlled by grasping, often absentee, landlords, who refused to guarantee the peasants tenure, even in their slim holdings. Forced to choose between emigration and starvation, many reluctantly chose to leave. But the wrench was painful; this initial phase of emigration attracted only the more desperate or ambitious souls.

A second phase began when those in America wrote home praising their new country, extolling the life they now enjoyed and urging their friends and relatives to join them. This last sentiment was constantly echoed; as one Irishman wrote of his brother, "Had I him here, I would count myself the happiest of men." Promotional literature supplemented such appeals. One clergyman maintained a library of approximately a thousand volumes of guidebooks and the like for prospective emigrants, while similar literature circulated throughout the country. Rev. J. O'Hanlon's *The Emigrant Guide for the United States,* published in Boston, proved very popular and useful.

The expatriates often enclosed in their letters of encouragement more tangible assistance. One contemporary estimated that the American Irish had forwarded over 24 million pounds to the old country in one five-year period. Although this figure may be an exaggerated one, the actual sum dispatched was probably considerable. According to a respectable estimate, the Irish of New York City alone sent $8 million in the famine year of 1846. Another observer noted, "The great ambition of the Irish girl is to send something to her people as soon as possible after she has landed in America; and in innumerable instances the first tidings of her arrival in the New World are accompanied with a remittance, the fruits of her first earnings in her first place."

Often, a father, arriving first, would begin immediately to save for his family's passage. In a letter from a husband to his wife, we find the awkwardness and the sketchy punctuation of his writing expressive of his emotion and expectancy: "Don't answer this letter til you receive the next in which money will be for you. Keep your heart as God spared you so long you will be shortly in the Lands of Promise and live happy with me and our children."

Another impulse to emigration developed after 1825, when the British government, which had previously limited the numbers of people leaving Ireland, changed its attitude, partly because of the warnings of Thomas Malthus and others on the dangers of overpopulation, but also because a policy of restriction proved difficult and expensive to enforce. In addition, after 1815, landlords found it steadily less profitable to keep tenants on small parcels of land. The ruinous agricultural depression following the end of the Napoleonic Wars hit Ireland especially hard; thousands of peasants making a marginal living even in good times defaulted on their land rents. This depression, added to legislation depriving the poorer renters of their votes (which the landlord controlled), and an increasing tax burden to provide for the destitute made it politically feasible for the landlords to evict those who could not pay and to help them to emigrate. Finally, all of the accumulated problems of injustice, discrimination, and overpopulation reached their climax in the potato famine, one of the great human disasters in history, a catastrophe that turned widespread emigration into frenzied evacuation.

Between 1841 and 1851, Ireland lost a population of at least two and one-half million. Famine, with its accompanying diseases of typhus, cholera, and relapsing fever, killed about a million people and drove another million and a half overseas. The cause of the famine was the potato blight, a frightening malady which destroyed the one absolutely essential item in the Irish diet. To understand the intensity of "the great hunger" one must appreciate the complete dependence of the peasant class on the potato. A wondrously cheap and easily cultivated food eaten by man and beast alike, it could be produced in large quantities on small plots of ground. An acre and a half provided a family of five or six with food for a year.

Yet it was a notoriously unreliable crop; many times in the past, blight had destroyed large portions of the crop in Ireland and elsewhere in Europe. All lived in dread of a universal failure, because there was simply no chance to produce enough of other foods to feed the island. For years afterward, those who had been Irish leaders during the famine were to recall with great rancor the indisputable fact that huge quantities of grain were taken from Ireland to England when the Irish peasantry were dying from starvation. At first glance, such action appears to have been incredibly inhuman; in subsequent studies, however, it has been demonstrated that the British sent more foodstuffs into Ireland during the famine than they took out.

In any event, the keeping of grain in the country would probably not have helped matters much. Irish cooking did not extend much beyond the different ways of preparing potatoes. Sir Charles Trevelyan, the British official charged with alleviating the distresses of the famine, complained, "There is scarcely a woman of the peasant class in the West of Ireland whose culinary art exceeds the boiling of a potato. Bread is scarcely ever seen, and an oven is unknown."

As a result, when the blight struck in 1845, it peremptorily cut off half of Ireland's supply of food. In a few days, throughout the country the great harvest from the ground had changed into tangles of corruption. But 1845 felt only a limited blight; the condition worsened with almost complete failures in 1846 and 1847 until misery overspread the country. Suffering beggars description: Hundreds of thousands died and millions lost their land. One compassionate landlord wrote:

This extensive district contains four parishes, with a population of 9800 souls [of which] there are at this moment over 7000 in the greatest state of misery and distress, out of which 5000 have not, unless given them, a single meal to provide for their wants tomorrow. This has arisen from the total failure of the potato, upon which the people solely relied . . . I am at this time giving food to a girl of twelve years old, the only remnant of a family, consisting of eight persons, her father and mother included, all of whom were alive one fortnight ago.

It is little wonder that to avoid the rising cost of the "poor taxes" brought on by the impoverishment of nearly the entire agricultural population, landlords offered to pay the passage of paupers to America. The impoverished peasants leaped at the opportunity: Over 870,000 went to America alone between 1846 and 1850. A human tide continued to flow; by 1860, more than 1,600,000 Irish lived in the United States. The famine had relaxed the peasant's anxious grip on his land: The last psychological barrier to emigration had been broken. Peasants sailed willingly now, without the "keen" or wailing with which the Irish customarily mourned their dead and their departing. And with them to the ships and their new country, they carried a legacy of rancor toward England, seeing her as the visible cause of their exile.

Americans often regard the Irish animosity toward Great Britain as something irrational, yet the experience of the famine makes the grievances understandable. The English historian Cecil Woodham-Smith, author of *The Great Hunger,* the most authoritative account of the famine, has charged that although the government in London did react with imagination and generosity in the early years of the blight, when the crisis became most acute, after 1847, and help was drastically needed, Britain, in effect, abandoned Ireland. She concludes that although one must make an effort not to judge the British government of the 1840s by standards of today (understanding that callous officials were not unusual in nineteenth-century Europe), it is difficult still to reconcile the action of the government with concepts of duty and moral principles.

Even leaders who made creditable records in social-reform and good government in Great Britain during the nineteenth century lost their patience and tolerance in dealing with the Irish. Blinded by centuries of religious antagonism and ethnic hostility, officials placed blame for the troubles upon the nature of the Irish themselves and not on the potato blight. "The great evil with which we have to contend," wrote Sir Charles Trevelyan, "is not the physical evil of the famine but the moral evil of the selfish, perverse and turbulent character of the people."

The Irish reciprocated in kind. The conciliatory counsel of one Irish statesman that "Irish history is for Ireland to forget and England to remember" was emphatically rejected by the Irish in the United States. British policy during the famine not only cut a new gulf between the English and the Irish, but it helped to embitter Anglo-American relations for more than half a century. Nothing could better insure an enthusiastic response and spirited support by Irish-Americans than a polemic against England; before long many an American politician would become adept at "pulling the lion's tail" and badgering "John Bull."

Sources

Adams, W. F., *Ireland and Irish Emigration to the New World from 1815 to the Famine*, New Haven, 1932.

Appel, John J., "The New England Origins of the American Irish Historical Society," *New England Quarterly*, Vol. XXXIII, No. 4, December 1960.

Churchill, Winston, *A History of the English Speaking Peoples*, Vol. II, *The New World*, New York, 1959.

Hansen, Marcus Lee, *The Atlantic Migration, 1607–1860*, Cambridge, 1940.

Smith, Abbot Emerson, *Colonists in Bondage: White Servitude and Convict Labor in America, 1607–1776*, Chapel Hill, N. C., 1947.

Woodham-Smith, Cecil, *The Great Hunger*, New York, 1962.

Chapter Three

The Struggle for Acceptance

One who comes in poverty to a strange land needs, above all, a capacity to endure. Immigrants to the United States are no exception. In this chapter, we shall see how the new Irish were exploited when they landed, how they were obliged to take menial, physically demanding jobs, and how their poor housing and incomes helped to breed crime and violence in their urban ghettos. The War between the States, as much as any single event, provided the Irish with an opportunity to distinguish themselves among their American comrades. Irish bravery on the battlefield diminished the fears—social, political, and economic—that the "paddies" had generated in the past.

Having made his way to a port city—Londonderry or Belfast in the north, Dublin in the east, Galway in the west, Waterford or Cork in the south—or perhaps, after an earlier voyage across the Irish Channel, to Liverpool or Glasgow, the Irish emigrant faced the terrors of the crossing. In the days of sailing ships—the greater part of the nineteenth century—most immigrant ships were really freight carriers, hurriedly "converted" to carry human cargo. Into the holds of these "damned plague ships and swimming coffins," rapacious owners crammed so many people that any semblance of privacy disappeared. Overcrowding and the absence of even rudimentary sanitary facilities helped spread diseases that had been carried aboard.

Although historians have perhaps exaggerated the incidence of disease-infested ships, it was the unhappy lot of the famine emigrants to take passage during the worst years, particularly 1848, the year of the frightful typhus epidemic. Of an estimated 100,000 people who made the voyage from the United Kingdom to various points in Canada, 17,000 died during the voyage and another 20,000 died after arrival. In New York, a doctor in the Staten Island

Quarantine Station who discovered on one ship 115 cases of typhus or Irish "famine fever" thought the Black Hole of Calcutta "a mercy compared with the holds of such vessels." At least, however, the Staten Island station provided a hospital for the suffering. No such facilities existed at Grosse Island, Quebec, where 84 ships were detained in a single year and thousands perished. An inscription in a Grosse Isle cemetery reads:

> In this secluded spot lie the mortal remains of 5,294 persons, who, flying from pestilence and famine in Ireland in the year 1847, found in America but a grave.

Nor did the navigational advances and improvements in shipbuilding entirely prevent the loss of vessels at sea. Some went down in sight of America. Henry David Thoreau, on his way to an exploration of Cape Cod in 1849, described the recovery of some of 145 bodies from the brig *St. John* out of Galway wrecked on the rocks off Cohasset, Massachusetts. "Why care for these dead bodies?" he wondered. "They really have no friends but the worms or fishes. Their owners were coming to the New World as Columbus did and the Pilgrims did—they were within a mile of its shores, but, before they could reach it, they emigrated to a newer world than Columbus ever dreamed of." In later years, the speed of the steamship mitigated the sufferings of the crossing, but travel in steerage still remained a severe endurance trial.

Upon debarkation, "runners" boarded the ship. Employed by hotels, boarding houses, or even saloons, these rough and dangerous men, "big-fisted shoulder hitters who pride themselves on travelling through life on their muscle," were usually the same nationality as the immigrants, but lived by exploiting them. Runners would offer to "take charge" of newcomers' luggage and to bring it to a boarding house for safe-keeping. Such houses prospered by tricking the immigrant, often overcharging him for meals or rooms and then taking his belongings in payment. A contemporary account detailed the tribulations of a young Irishman landing in New York in 1848:

> The moment he landed, his luggage was pounced upon by two runners, one seizing the box of tools, the other confiscating the clothes. The future American citizen assured his obliging friends that he was quite capable of carrying his own luggage; but no, they should relieve him—the stranger, and guest of the Republic—of that trouble. Each was in the interest of a different boarding house, and each insisted that the young Irishman with the red head should go with him. . . . Not being able to oblige both gentlemen, he could oblige only one; and as the tools were more valuable than the clothes, he followed the gentleman who had secured that portion of the "plunder." . . . The two gentlemen wore very pronounced green neck-ties, and spoke with a richness of accent that denoted special if not conscientious cultivation; and on his [the Irishman's] arrival at the boarding house, he was cheered with the announcement that its proprietor was from "the ould country, and loved every sod of it, God bless it!"

Another common fraud practiced by the runners involved the sale of passage tickets to different parts of the country. The immigrant, shown a printed ticket with a picture of a steamboat or a railroad, believes he has purchased comfortable transportation to his destination. Only after he has commenced his journey does he discover either that his ticket is good only for part of the distance, or that his accommodations have been changed, or that he must pay exorbitant freight charges.

A large number of those who came in at the port cities got no further. Some of the earlier Irish immigrants, those who had been lucky enough to migrate with a little money, had purchased a homestead on the frontier, but the peasants of the famine exodus remained in the city of debarkation or went to another, despite considerable efforts to persuade them to leave it. From the first, Irish-American leaders cried out against the dangers of the city. Thomas D'arcy McGee found it impossible to understand why "a people who in Ireland hungered and thirsted for land, who struggled for conacre and cabin even to the shedding of blood, when they reached the New World, in which a day's wages would purchase an acre of wild land in fee, wilfully concurred . . . to sink into the condition of a miserable town tenantry, to whose squalor even the European seaports would hardly present a parallel." In April 1850, the *Catholic Telegraph and Advocate* of Cincinnati warned: "A strong active Irishman might as well commence digging his own grave, as to shut himself up in one of our large cities. . . . Fly from the large cities as from a plague."

Father O'Hanlon's *Emigrant Guide* encouraged settlement in the countryside and warned of the snares the unsuspecting newcomers faced in the cities. In the 1830s, Bishop Benedict Fenwick of Boston established an agricultural settlement for immigrant Irish at Benedicta, Maine. Later, two constant critics of the conditions and quality of urban life, Bishop Mathias Loras of Dubuque and Andrew Byrne of Little Rock, attempted without much success to attract the immigrants to rural Arkansas and Iowa. Such efforts to colonize the Irish in a rural environment would continue into the twentieth century. Writing in the 1880s of what he called "the religious mission of the Irish people," Bishop John Lancaster Spalding of Peoria, Illinois, put the case that only the farmer could be a free man, politically and economically. Altering its position of the earlier years of immigration, when Archbishop John Hughes, among others, criticized rural colonization schemes as a threat to the religious solidarity of the Irish, the Catholic hierarchy accepted Spalding's contention that "the agricultural life more than that of the city conduces to happiness and morality, and that it harmonizes better with the Christian ideal." Still nothing much in the way of tangible settlements came out of Spalding's preaching of the rural religious mission.

Indeed, a sizable number of those initially settled on the land soon gravitated back to the cities. Carl Wittke, the eminent historian of immigration, has speculated about what might have been, had the Irish continued to live on the land in America as they had in the old country: "What a difference it might have made, and what an excellent investment it might have turned out to be, had the government used its funds to transport the Irish into the West and helped them to become established farmers on the public lands!"

True, the lack of the necessary money to buy land, tools, seed, and transportation to the West kept many of the Irish, especially those who fled the famine, in the places where they came off the boats. Nonetheless, it remains doubtful that government subsidies could have induced any substantial number to the frontier. The experience of the famine had created among the Celts a deep cultural and social aversion to agriculture. To the Irishman, the land had become a symbol of oppression; for him, farming did not connote the Jeffersonian image of the noble yeoman enjoying abundance, independence, and contentment. Rather it meant poverty, long, arduous, unrewarding labor, dependence on an alien master and, possibly, starvation and eviction. Even the pleasant scenes they retained of rural life in Ireland, images of neighborliness and warmth, could not be conjured in the vast, strange setting of America.

An Irish farmer in Missouri in fact boasted about the heralded advantages of American agriculture, "land and stock, no rent, light taxes and whiskey without government inspection, free shooting and, above all, social equality" —yet he missed the camaraderie of Irish life:

I could then go to a fair, a wake or a dance, or I would spend the winter nights in a neighbour's house, cracking the jokes by the turf fire. I had there but a sore head, I would have a neighbour within every hundred yards of me that would run to see me. But here everyone can get so much land, that they calls them neighbours that lives two or three miles off—*och sorra* take such neighbours I would say. And then I would sit down and cry and curse him who made me leave home.

Longing for the companionship of his fellow folk and needing the consolations of religion, the Irish immigrant stayed in the cities. Despite their peasant background, or perhaps because of it, the Irish in the United States were temperamentally unsuited to farm life. Finally—and this last reason was the ruling consideration with most men—the city offered opportunities: jobs at first, and political power later. Budding Irish politicians realized the voting power that lay in the crowded Irish towns. Thinning out across the frontier could only dilute this incipient power. "Paddy would never leave the city," complained one nativist critic. "They would then lose the glory of having a Paddy O'Bluster in one office, a Rory McWhackem in another, a Tammany Batterscull in a third."

Thus did former peasants of Ireland become an urban proletariat. They crowded together in tenements or in wood-and-tarpaper shanties in neighborhoods where the earlier Irish had already established themselves. Whether in New York's "Five Points" district, or Boston's North End, or New Orleans' "Irish Channel," living conditions for the famine generation were appallingly similar. Quick to exploit the ceaseless demand for cheap housing, builders used every inch of space in the Irish slums to squeeze in another flimsy tenement; such density of squalid building made it impossible to chart the streets of such areas. The compiler of the first Boston atlas curtly described the Irish ghettos as "full of sheds and shanties."

Into one of these human rookeries, upwards of twenty families would be caged; in some instances families of seven or eight, or even two families, "shared" a single room. All space within was used for habitation, from stifling attics in which it was impossible for a man to stand, to dank cellars where air and light hardly ever penetrated. A physician investigating the sanitary conditions of New York City's laboring population in 1844 found two families, ten persons in all, occupying a cellar ten feet square and eleven feet high! He discovered another cellar built against the wall of a churchyard with moisture draining in, "and the musty smell which exudes from the clothes of the persons inhabiting the cellar is unmistakable."

A luckier family might possess the luxury of a window, but it often opened upon a backyard outhouse, the stench from which kept the window closed. A health committee in Boston found an Irish district to be

a perfect hive of human beings, without comforts and mostly without common necessaries; in many cases huddled together like brutes without regard to age or sex or sense of decency; grown men and women sleeping together in the same apartment and sometimes wife and husband, brothers and sisters in the same bed. Under such circumstances self-respect, forethought, all the high and noble virtues soon die out and sullen indifference and despair, or disorder, intemperance and utter degradation reign supreme.

Despair indeed led to "disorder" and "intemperance." Whiskey, formerly a popular peasant drink in Irish homes and farms, now became an anodyne that gave the Irish laborer temporary relief from the bleakness of his condition. The grog shop or saloon, often located in a cellar among the living quarters, served as the center of the ghetto life and provided the sociability craved by the displaced Irish. Inevitably, heavy drinking led to brawling and the Irishman was soon classified as an offensive, lawbreaking drunkard. To combat the vice, Father Theobald Mathew of Cork, a renowned temperance advocate, came to America to preach his doctrine of teetotalism and to help his countrymen "snap their chains of enslavement to liquor." He succeeded in getting thousands to take the pledge, but never had any real chance of entirely eliminating whiskey consumption. For too many it had become almost a necessity, the easy way to purchase forgetfulness for these denizens of America's first slums, a liquid drug that helped, they thought, to cope with their degradation.

Yet poverty alone does not provide an adequate explanation for the "curse of the Irish." It has endured into the age of affluence. According to a recent study by John L. Thomas, a Jesuit sociologist who conducted a survey of the records of the Chicago Archdiocese's marriage court, alcoholism frequently causes disruptions of Irish-American marriages. In *Beyond the Melting Pot,* Nathan Glazer and Daniel P. Moynihan conclude that "a good deal of competent enquiry has still not produced much understanding of the Irish tendency to alcohol addiction. . . . A dominant social fact of the Irish community is the number of good men who are destroyed by drink."

From his human warren, the immigrant went out in search of a job, and he usually found it at the bottom of the occupational ladder. In a pattern followed by the Italians and the Poles who came later in the nineteenth century and the Negroes and Puerto Ricans of recent years, the Irish were "hewers of wood and drawers of water." They took menial jobs only the unskilled applied for: hod carrier, street cleaner, longshoreman, day laborer. Thanks to Professor Oscar Handlin's seminal study, *Boston Immigrants,* we have fairly accurate statistics on the occupations of the famine Irish. In the Boston of the 1840s, 48 percent of the city's Irish-born, 7007 of 14,895, were unskilled day laborers. Among other Boston groups, only the Negroes and the Germans had as much as 10 percent of their population working as laborers, and the actual number was infinitesimal: 115 Negroes and 107 Germans.

Domestic service ranked next in number of employed. Of necessity, Irish women worked; their employers found them to be excellent servants, bringing good sense, blithe attitudes, and quiet loyalty to their low-paying positions. Bridget or Kate cooking in the kitchen were as familiar as Pat or Mike digging a ditch. By 1850, at a conservative estimate, 2227 Irish girls worked as domestic servants in Boston alone. Providing, as it usually did, three meals a day and warm lodgings, domestic service remained a popular calling for immigrant girls for many years. In *Advice to Irish Girls in America,* a sturdy homily written in 1872, readers were asked to recall that even saints were servants and that domestics performed tasks not unlike those of guardian angels!

The United States had a seemingly inexhaustible demand for cheap menial labor, and Ireland provided it with her sons and daughters. As one newspaper put it, "There are several sorts of power working at the fabric of this Republic —waterpower, steampower and Irish power. The last works hardest of all." In antebellum America, Irish labor made possible the expansion of old cities and the founding of new ones. To build streets, dig sewers, construct water systems, the Irish were called upon. At the same time, the abundance of immigrant labor stimulated manufacturing, for it did not take the entrepreneurs of Jacksonian America long to entice the cheap Irish labor into their booming factories and expanding transportation networks. Factory owners considered the immigrant a much more docile and satisfactory worker than the native American. The textile mill operators of Lowell and Lawrence, whose original source of labor had been young ladies from the farms of rural New England, now turned to the Irish, who were so obviously solicitous for work and therefore usually more reliable and cooperative than Yankee girls, some of whom had been joining the Female Labor Reform Association. By 1860, the Irish were nearly half of Lowell's population.

More often than not, when the Irish immigrant left the Atlantic cities, he left on a labor contract. Newspapers carried column after column of advertising describing jobs available: work on the railroads, on canals, or in the mines. By 1850, Boston had assumed the role of national labor reservoir; the city's Irish newspapers published advertisements in single issues for a total of 2000 men wanted in widely scattered places. Unable to resist the blandishments of steady employment and the promise of good wages and excellent food and lodgings, thousands replied. The social historian J. C. Furnas suggests that for single men the railroad and canal-making had special attractions. He cites the report of the French economist Michel Chevalier, who had found an Irish railroad gang earning 75 cents a day, with lodging and meals, including bread, butter, meat, and coffee, and six to eight drinks of whiskey. In France, such work brought 24 cents a day and "feed yourself." A worker writing to his relatives in Ireland declared that he ate meat three times a week. Why did he say this, he was asked, when he really enjoyed meat three times a day? "Because," answered the Irishman, "if I told them that, they'd never believe me."

Chevalier's example, unfortunately, is the exception to the rule: Most of the railroad and canal workers fell victim to avaricious subcontractors who charged more for necessary supplies than what the unsuspecting greenhorn earned. Many a man arrived in a railroad camp hundreds of miles from his home only to discover that the company had advertised for many more workers than it needed and offered less than it promised. What choice did the destitute worker have but to accept the lower offer? The *Boston Pilot* thought the railroads had been "the ruin of thousands of our poor people," and urged "all laborers who can get employment elsewhere to avoid the railroads, to do anything in fact in preference to railroading." When entire families followed the progress of the roads, the wretched conditions in the seaboard cities invariably reappeared. In *American Notes,* Charles Dickens has recorded his revulsion after observing a colony of Irish railroad builders in upstate New York in 1841:

With means at hand of building decent cabins, it was wonderful to see how clumsy, rough, and wretched, its hovels were. The best were poor protection from the weather; the worst let in the wind and rain through the wide breaches in the roofs of sodden grass, and in the walls of mud; some had neither door nor window; some had nearly fallen down, and were imperfectly propped up by stakes and poles; all were ruinous and filthy. Hideously ugly old women and very buxom young ones, pigs, dogs, men, children, babies, pots, kettles, dunghills, vile refuse, rank straw and standing water, all wallowing together in an inseparable heap, composed the furniture of every dark and dirty hut.

Years of Irish work in building a new transportation system helped, to an extent, to fan out their population, and the Irishman soon became a familiar figure in every section of the country. Even in the South, sizable Celtic communities blossomed in Charleston, Mobile, New Orleans, and St. Louis. Others found their way to Ohio, Indiana, Illinois, Wisconsin, and across the Mississippi into Iowa. Akron, Ohio, began as an Irish railroad shantytown; cities as geographically disparate as Albany and Peoria, Buffalo and Omaha, soon had their "Paddy's Quarter," "Irishtown," or "Irish Channel."

Weakening physical labor coalesced with virulent living conditions to make Irish slums breeding grounds for disease (tuberculosis was so common that for many years it was called the Irish disease), and many a newcomer found a premature grave in America. One English traveller mused: "Heaven knows how many poor Hibernians have been consumed and buried in these Louisianian swamps, leaving their earnings to the dramshop keeper and the contractor, and the results of their toil to the planter." In Boston, on an average, the Irish died only 14 years after reaching the city, but, ironically, this figure represented a longer life expectancy than in Ireland, where the average age at death was 19, and where four out of five people did not live to be 40 years of age.

Such statistics dramatize the paradox of the immigrant. No matter how full of struggle life in America was, it was admittedly better than it had been in Ireland. To live in Lowell, Massachusetts, for example, cramped in odorous tenements, laboring from daybreak till dusk for a weekly pittance, seeing one's son or daughter perfunctorily file into factory death traps while yet in childhood, is hardly the ideal of a decent existence. "But Lowell was a damn sight better than County Cork," observes the historian of social mobility, Stephan Thernstrom, "and men who knew from bitter experience what County Cork was like could not view their life in Lowell with quite the same simple revulsion as the middle-class reformers who judged Lowell by altogether different standards."

How antipathy toward the Irish affected American politics is discussed in following chapters. The formation of the American or Know-Nothing Party about 1850 merely helped to organize anti-immigrant and anti-Catholic prejudice, and the ultimate decline of political nativism did not measurably improve the status of the Irish. Continuing *Irishphobia*, in fact, caused some concern when the Civil War erupted upon the nation.

After the firing on Fort Sumter, when Abraham Lincoln called for volunteers to suppress the rebellion a fear spread that the Irish would be slow to respond. Would they not harbor a resentment over the prejudice directed against them during the previous decade? Would not their anti-abolitionism make them less than enthusiastic about a war against the slaveholders? "We hear on all sides the sounds of disunion," a critic of nativism had warned: "Supposing it should come, and that Massachusetts stood alone, can she . . . expect that these men, who she is now about to proscribe, will rush to her assistance?"

But the Irish did rush to assist their adopted country. They had come to prize the Union and the Constitution. When Beauregard's cannon fired upon the flag at Sumter, the Southern secessionists immediately took the place of the radical New England abolitionists as the chief threat to the preservation of the Union. Observed the New York *Irish American,* "Secession means revolution; there can be no doubt of this; and we cannot be induced to forswear the allegiance we have pledged to our adopted country to gratify the secessionists, by abetting them in their unwise and anti-national proceedings." Moreover, the apparent sympathy of Great Britain for the Southern cause gave the war the character of a good scrap with the ancient enemy.

A more prosaic factor was also involved: Bounties paid to enlistees, amounting to $500 or $600 or more, proved a tempting lure to many a poor Irishman. During the war the Confederates charged the Union government with actively recruiting soldiers in Ireland and Germany, using cash bounties as bait. A Confederate agent in Europe complained that the jails and poor-houses had been swept clean by recruiting agents. Recruiters reminded Irish youths of the invaluable military training they would acquire: It would prove useful in the "coming struggle" for Irish freedom. Although the total number of men obtained for the Union ranks in this manner is difficult to estimate, it probably ran into the tens of thousands. A. Dudley Mann, in a special Confederate mission to Rome, persuaded Pope Pius IX to discourage Federal recruitment in Ireland, but the papal intervention did not substantially decrease the number of enlistments.

Estimates of native sons of Erin serving in the Union armies range from 150,000 to 200,000, with New York furnishing the largest number of regiments among the famous Irish Brigade. This group was commanded by an exiled revolutionary, Thomas F. Meagher, who was referred to, somewhat grandiloquently, as "Meagher of the Sword." Other large contingents came from Massachusetts, Michigan, Ohio, Indiana, Illinois, and Iowa. Horace Greeley's *New York Tribune* exulted, "The Irish spirit of the North is thoroughly aroused."

Irishmen soon gained almost universal admiration for their reckless courage; in desperate situations generals often looked first to their Celtic warriors. Lloyd Lewis in his stirring biography of William Tecumseh Sherman writes of the battle of First Bull Run:

Sherman turned and called to his Irish. It was a medieval movement . . . long lines of men on scarlet knees in green grass . . . a strange green banner above them . . .bayonets glittering like spears above their bowed heads . . . Latin words rolling from the lips of Father O'Reilly, who commended every soul to God. The benediction done, the men put on their caps, and as they rose, Captain Meagher, standing in front, ran his eye up and down the line and then in fond challenge cried, "Come on, boys, you've got your chance at last." Ten little drummers fluttered their sticks. The regiment leaped forward shouting an Old World battle cry, "For Ireland and Fontenoy!"

Far fewer Irish lived in the slave states, but those who did responded generously to the call of the Confederacy, becoming the most numerous of all the nationalities in the rebel armies. Two companies of the New Orleans Irish, the Montgomery Guards and the Emmett Guards, helped form the First Louisiana Regiment. The Emerald Guards of Mobile attired themselves in green to honor their homeland. Texas and North Carolina also contributed companies composed almost exclusively of Irishmen. A historian of the Southern armies described them as often rough, quarrelsome, and impervious to discipline, "but blessed with a redeeming good humor and enjoying a universal reputation as good fighters." General Patrick Cleburne of County Cork rose to Major-General in the Confederate armies, was several times cited for valor, and earned the sobriquet "Stonewall Jackson of the West" before being killed in action in 1864.

A tradition of Irish gallantry, élan, and love of battle endured into later wars. The fighting Irishman became a famous stereotype; there were no scrappers quite like the Irish, all "honest men, with broad shoulders and a knockout in each fist." In 1898, American newspapermen trying to locate the first soldier to reach the blockhouse on San Juan Hill felt sure that he would be "a red-haired Irishman" and were disappointed when he turned out to be an utterly ordinary American of German ancestry. And in a biography of "Wild Bill" Donovan published in 1970, when martial glory had lost some of its allure, author Corey Ford nonetheless retains the old clichés. As a young man, Donovan "like any boy, had the dream of leading an Irish regiment into battle, though he never could have guessed in his wildest dreams that one day he would command the bravest of them all, the Fighting Irish of New York."

Sources

Arensberg, Conrad, *The Irish Countryman: An Anthropological Study,* New York, 1937.

Blegen, Theodore C., Editor, *Land of Their Choice: The Immigrants Write Home,* Minneapolis, 1955.

Dickens, Charles, *American Notes,* London, 1842.

Ernst, Robert, *Immigrant Life in New York City, 1825–1863,* New York, 1949.

Furnas, J. C., *The Americans: A Social History of the United States, 1587-1914,* New York, 1969.

Handlin, Oscar, *Boston's Immigrants: A Study in Acculturation,* Revised Edition, Cambridge, Mass., 1959.

Lewis, Lloyd, *Sherman: Fighting Prophet,* New York, 1932.

Lonn, Ella, *Foreigners in the Confederacy,* Chapel Hill, N. C., 1940.

————, *Foreigners in the Union Army and Navy,* Baton Rouge, 1951.

Maguire, John F., *The Irish in America,* London, 1868.

Potter, George W., *To the Golden Door: The Story of the Irish in Ireland and America,* Boston, 1960.

Shannon, James P., *Catholic Colonization on the Western Frontier,* New Haven, 1957.

Thernstrom, Stephan, "Urbanization, Migration, and Social Mobility in Late Nineteenth Century America," in Barton J. Bernstein, Editor, *Towards a New Past: Dissenting Essays in American History,* New York, 1969.

A priest blesses a group about to migrate from Ireland to America (1851).

Heavy immigrant representation on railroad construction crews included many Irish (Pacific Railroad, 1869).

Three expressions of domestic animosity to the popular stereotype of the Irishman, by the prominent newspaper editorial cartoonist Thomas Nast.

THE GREEK SLAVE.

April 16, 1870

December 9, 1876

The Ignorant Vote—Honors Are Easy.

Four views of immigrant circumstances in late nineteenth-century New York City.

Bandit's Roost, Mulberry Street

Photograph by Jacob A. Riis. The Jacob A. Riis Collection, Museum of the City of New York

Mullen's Alley

Photograph by Jacob A. Riis. The Jacob A. Riis Collection, Museum of the City of New York

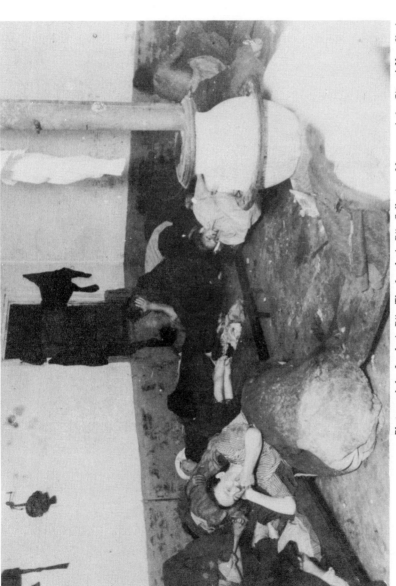

Photograph by Jacob A. Riis, The Jacob A. Riis Collection, Museum of the City of New York

Police station lodging room for women, lower east side

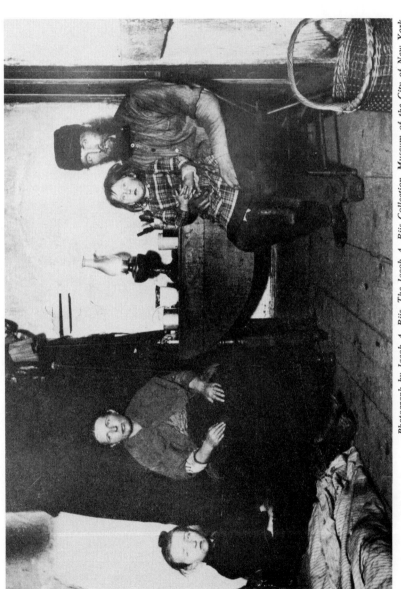

Tenement interior in Poverty Gap

Chapter Four

Getting into the Mainstream

The honors and promotions the Irish garnered on the battlefields of the Civil War quickly showed their countrymen that they were acceptable men of war. And in other areas of life—in racial, economic, political, and cultural matters—progress for the Irish was in many ways as difficult and rife with battle as the war itself. One might describe these "adolescent" years as a catalogue of animus among the Irish toward the blacks, the "unionizing" of anti-Irish sentiment in the Know-Nothing Party, the grim story of the Molly Maguires, the rise of the Irish political tradition in benevolent and protective associations, and the blossoming of an Irish contribution to popular culture and, eventually, genuine artistic accomplishment.

Throughout the antebellum years the Irish lingered on the low rung of the work ladder. Those seeking better jobs read with loathing the familiar notice: "No Irish need apply." They continued their rivalry with the slaves of the South or the free Negroes of the North for the most menial jobs. Travelers in the Southern states often noted the widespread employment of Irish immigrants, not slaves, whenever there was any dangerous or unpleasant work to be done. On a journey through the seaboard slave states in the early 1850s, Frederick Law Olmstead asked a Virginia planter why he employed Irishmen on a drainage project rather than his own hands. "It's dangerous work," the planter replied, "and a negro's life is too valuable to be risked at it. If a negro dies, it is a considerable loss, you know." Later on his trip, Olmstead watched a gang of Irish roustabouts load a cotton boat on the Alabama River. He wondered why slaves stood at the top of the chute while the Irish were stationed at its bottom to catch the wildly careening bales of cotton. The astute captain explained, "The niggers are worth too much to be risked here; if the Paddies are knocked overboard, or get their backs broke, nobody loses anything." At one point, such exploitation of cheap immigrant labor became so pronounced as to provoke Bishop John England of Charleston, South Carolina, to warn the Irish against settling in the South.

Given such a situation, Irish antagonism toward the blacks was predictable. Quite apart from a desire to maintain his meagre status, for the immigrant at least outranked the Negro on the social pyramid, wary Irishmen in slave states feared the competition that emancipation of the blacks would bring. In his entire experience, Olmstead had discovered no native Southerners who exceeded "in idolatry to Slavery the mass of ignorant, foreign-born laborers. Their hatred of the negro is proportionate to the equality of their intellect and character to his; and their regard for Slavery to their disinclination to compete with him in a fair field."

In the free states, similar hostility between Irish and black was engendered when the two groups found themselves pitted against each other for the pick-and-shovel jobs on road gangs, canals, and railroads. Employers often deliberately encouraged such antagonisms, for the same reasons that some of America's present ethnic rivalries have been exploited; on occasion, blacks were brought in to break Irish-led strikes. As a result of measures taken against them, the Irish reacted angrily to talk of abolishing slavery: They feared emancipated workers would flood the cheap-labor market. Psychologists have argued that it takes a reasonably contented man to interest himself in the problems of others. Totally concerned with his own precarious livelihood, the Irish worker had nothing but contempt for abolitionist leaders like Wendell Phillips who worried about the welfare of slaves in faraway Mississippi while opposing labor organizations in Massachusetts.

Other factors contributed to Celtic antiabolitionism. The same reformers who carried the antislavery standard usually espoused the cause of temperance, a euphemism for the total prohibition of alcoholic beverages. To the hard-drinking Irish, such a proposal was little short of insane, as well as a slur on their social customs.

Also (and such appears to have been particularly so in Massachusetts), the leading abolitionists were almost exclusively of Protestant, Federalist descent, and therefore, by definition, antagonistic to Irish Catholic Democrats: Had not some of them openly identified themselves with nativism? Then too, their intemperate attacks on the Constitution, which William Lloyd Garrison called "a covenant with death and an agreement with hell," offended the politically conservative leaders of the Catholic Church. To the famous convert and Catholic spokesman Orestes Brownson, the abolitionists posed a danger to a stable society by agitating too much about slavery. If the slaves had a master who "is a true Christian, and takes care that his people are instructed and brought up in the true Christian faith, and worship, slavery is tolerable, and for negroes, perhaps, even more than tolerable."

Very few Irish saw any conflict between agitating for freedom in Ireland and defending human slavery in the United States. From time to time, antislaveryites tried to persuade the Irish that the slave system threatened the status of free laborers. "American slavery," resolved the Massachusetts Anti-Slavery Society in 1843, "is the deadliest foe of the rights of labor, and ought, therefore to be the object of special indignation and alarm to the hard-working Irish immigrant."

All was to no avail, however, for even an appeal to oppose slavery from the famous and beloved Daniel O'Connell, champion of Irish freedom, fell on deaf ears. Typical of the prevailing attitude was that of the Irish editor who warned his readers not to jeopardize "the present freedom of a nation of white men for the vague forlorn hope of elevating blacks to a level for which it is at least problematical whether God and nature ever intended them." Such sentiments differed only in degree from those expressed by the defenders of slavery in the South; yet, in the South, the Irish came under the suspicion of those who viewed unrestricted immigration as a real threat to sectional political balance. With their growing population, the free states would ultimately be in a position to act directly against slavery. Despite the antiabolitionism of the Irish, a Mississippi Senator in 1853 believed "the whole education of foreigners and their prejudices when they came to this country are against the institution of slavery and everything they hear at the North confirms that prejudice."

Unhappily, even the Irishman's enthusiasm for the Union cause in the Civil War did not dissipate traditional Irish antipathy toward the black man. A popular doggerel ran:

> To the flag we are pledged—all its foes we abhor—
> And we ain't for the "nigger" but are for the war.

Prominent Irish-Americans openly opposed the Emancipation Proclamation, while the Negrophobia of the working class manifested itself in the ugly draft riots of 1863. The riots resulted from the passage of the Conscription Act of March 1863, which stated that all "able-bodied males between 20 and 45" were liable for military service, except that a man who was drafted could be excused if he provided an "acceptable substitute" or paid the government $300. Clearly an incompetent legislative blunder, the act provoked widespread national furor, the most serious of which occurred in New York City. For several days (July 13–16, 1863) a mob of immigrant laborers rampaged through the city, intimidating police and militia. Much of the mob's fury fell upon the Negroes, regarded as being responsible for the war, and, once emancipated, threatening intense job competition for the proletarian Irish. The use of blacks to break a recent longshoreman's strike in the city confirmed the worst fears of the workers. Throughout the several days of lawlessness, the crowd searched out unfortunate blacks, beating many and hanging several. A most senseless atrocity took place when the colored orphan asylum was set afire and destroyed. A company of Irish firemen and others managed to lead the two hundred or so orphans to safety.

The New York 7th Regiment (which had fought at Gettysburg), the naval forces, and the cadets of West Point joined police and militia in restoring order, but not until over a thousand people had been killed or injured and damage had reached an estimated two million dollars.

Some interesting parallels may be drawn between the long hot summer of 1863 in New York and the disturbances that struck various cities in the 1960s. Like black people today, many Irish had suffered alienation, a feeling that poverty only intensified. The provisions of the conscription legislation were obviously prejudical to their poverty, for one did not have to serve if he could purchase a substitute or make the payment. This description led to the understandable slogan "a rich man's war and a poor man's fight." (Because college students had been deferred from service, this was essentially the same indictment that black militant leaders leveled against the Vietnam war.) To the *New York Times,* one letter-writer wrote,

You will no doubt be hard on the rioters tomorrow morning. But the $300 law had made us nobodies, vagabonds and cast-outs of society for whom nobody cares. We are the poor rabble and the rich rabble is our enemy by this law. Although we got hard fists and are dirty without, we have soft hearts and clean consciences within, and that's the reason we love our children more than the rich, because we got not much besides them and will not leave them to starve.

As in recent times, it proved more satisfying for those who had engaged in bias to overlook the true causes of the rioting and to place blame upon "outside agitators." To the *Times* it was abundantly manifest that the whole affair was concocted on Sunday last by a few wire-pullers who, after they saw the ball in motion, prudently kept in the background," while the *New York Tribune* impugned the "niggerhead and copperhead press." Several journalists repeated an entirely unsubstantiated rumor that the riot was part of a "conspiracy" to aid the Confederacy, timed to coincide with Lee's invasion of the North. It is logical that Confederate agents in the city should do their best to keep the disorders going once they had begun, but once unloosed, the fury of the rootless poor of the city needed little stimulation. In our own day, in the popular mythology about civil disorders, "Communist sympathizers" working among the blacks may be compared to the "Confederate agents" stirring up the Irish. And, just as the angry Irish sought a scapegoat in the Negro, many of the dispossessed in our own black ghettos, using catch-all terms, have lashed out at Jewish storekeepers, as a handy symbol of their oppression.

The last decade of the antebellum period had witnessed the high-water mark of nativistic feeling against the Irish. One aspect of this hostility was rooted in differences in religion, inasmuch as many Americans viewed Protestant Americans as the culminating triumph of the Reformation, and readily believed the warnings of Samuel F. B. Morse, the painter-inventor, that most of the immigrants were Jesuits in disguise and that the Pope planned to move the Vatican to the Mississippi Valley! Such believers eagerly swallowed the sensationalism and thinly veiled pornography of the book described as the "Uncle Tom's Cabin" of the nativist movement, Maria Monk's *Awful Disclosures of the Hotel*

Dieu Convent of Montreal or the Secrets of Nunnery Revealed. This classic of anti-Catholicism would prove to be remarkably long lived; it circulated as recently as the 1960 presidential campaign. Unfortunately, Catholic leaders at times rubbed the raw wounds of religious bigotry by talking of the Catholic "mission" in America and bragging of conversions. Those skeptical enough to discredit Morse's creation of a Papal conspiracy were nonetheless alarmed at the pressures exerted by Bishop John Hughes of New York for support of parochial schools, and accordingly feared for the future of the public system. *Citizen,* an Irish weekly journal, admitted that "the ultra-Catholic journals went far beyond the bounds of prudence in writing on religious subjects."

And is it not logical that the Irish were detested by the working classes, whose jobs they threatened or whose standard of living they depressed by their willingness to work for low wages? Others embraced nativism from a real apprehension of the country's future if immigration were to remain unchecked. These Irish appeared to be unassimilable. George Templeton Strong, the epitome of the "proper" New Yorker of the pre-Civil War period, wrote: "Our Celtic fellow citizens are almost as remote from us in temperament and constitution as the Chinese." Unsavory Irish-American ghettos repelled observers; puritanical coteries reacted angrily to any drunkenness. The ghetto cycle was working: People who live poorly and are badly treated often turn to rowdiness and crime.

Men began to quote figures on the "foreign menace." In 1850, 20 percent of the native-born attended schools, compared to less than seven percent of the immigrants; aliens with scarcely more than one tenth of the population accounted for over half of the crimes. In New York City, the Irish contributed almost two thirds of the population of the charitable and penal institutions; they had turned respectable sections of American cities into slums, multiplied the grog houses and the saloons, made the streets "unsafe": What had happened to law and order in this country?

Perhaps dreaded even more than immigrant criminality was the spectre of political domination by the foreign-born. How long could Boston, for example, remain a Brahmin bastion when the Irish population increased about 200 percent between 1850 and 1855, while the number of native-born grew only by 15 percent? The leading historian of the nativist uproar noted, "To the men and women witnessing these changes there seemed more truth than wit in the tale of the schoolboy, who, when asked to parse "America" replied, "America is a very common noun, singular number, masculine gender, critical case, and governed by the Irish!"

In the post-Civil War years, Americans seemed to hold ambivalent attitudes toward the Irish. Their demonstrated loyalty to the Union engendered warm feelings, but it was easy to accept the stereotype of the comic Irishman, the merry, happy-go-lucky, boisterous Paddy, generally lovable but on occasion prone to take a drop too much and then liable to become troublesome. Professional Irishmen willing to play this caricature abounded, just as some blacks had been willing to play the Sambo role assigned to them in the slave system. In this way, the Irish could be tolerated, while being kept at an arm's length.

As Thomas Beer observed, "The Irish were at once established as tremendously funny, gay, and charming people and concurrently were snubbed."

This snobbery was especially true of leaders of the Republican Party. The enrollment of large numbers of former Know-Nothings in the Grand Old Party had the unfortunate effect of giving it a nativist tinge that lasted for a long generation. Predilections of the Irish for the Democratic Party intensified this bias, and leaders of the party originally formed to fight the oppression of the Negro now condoned and delighted in the fanatical virulence of cartoonist Thomas Nast, who drew the Irish as simian-faced brutes whose great ambition was to establish a priest-ridden despotism in America.

But Nast's pictures represented only one level of this prejudice. The historian James Ford Rhodes discussed the "hereditary bent" of the Irish toward incest, murder, and rape, and a future president of the United States, Rutherford B. Hayes, did not find it incongruous to deplore one kind of stupidity while encouraging another: "The Negro prejudice is rapidly wearing away," he wrote, "but is still strong among the Irish, and people of Irish parentage and the ignorant and unthinking generally."

Irish demands for public funds for Catholic schools and sporadic eruptions of violence boosted resentment. The *New York Times* in February 1871 protested the large amounts of money being granted to the Roman Catholic Church by city and state governments, and asked, "How Long Will Protestants Endure?" When Irish organizations threatened to disrupt a parade of Protestant Irish, or Orangemen, in New York in commemoration of the Battle of the Boyne (in which the forces of William of Orange in 1690 defeated the Irish Catholic troops of James II), the mayor of New York, A. Oakley Hall, promptly prohibited the parade. So great was the reaction to this surrender that the Governor of New York countermanded the order, allowing the parade to take place. This reversal led to the worst of a series of so-called "Orange riots" on July 12, 1871, because the Irish carried out their promise to break up the Orangemen's celebration. When it was over, 41 citizens and four policemen or soldiers lay dead and over 80 were wounded. New Yorkers pondered whether or not the Irish could ever be assimilated.

Nor was Irish violence confined to New York. Dennis Kearney's Workingman Party in San Francisco also caused alarm over "the wild Irish," but the most sensational incidents involved the Molly Maguires of the Pennsylvania coal fields. Jobs in the anthracite coal region of eastern Pennsylvania had attracted many Irish. Anthracite is finished now, but in the middle of the nineteenth century it was just coming into its own as the chief source of heat for homes and factories. As the demand for coal grew with an expanding economy and population, the need for workers did also, and the Irish would be followed to the mines by successive waves of immigrant peoples: Poles, Italians, Czechs, and Hungarians. The coal-carrying railroads that controlled the industry brutally exploited these workers. Skimpy wages, incredibly long hours, and atrocious working conditions routinely brought thousands of unhappy lives to untimely deaths. Some went gratefully. An epitaph on a miner's grave reads:

Forty years I worked with pick and drill
Down in the mines against my will
The coal King's slave but now its passed
Thanks be to God I am free at last.

Against this background the drama of the Molly Maguires was played out. Operating under the cover of a fraternal society, the Ancient Order of Hibernians, the Maguires struck out violently at the mine operators. Collieries were dynamited, unpopular foremen assassinated, and homes burned. The violence of the organization terrified the region and brought a blanket denunciation down upon the heads of the Irish.

Eventually, James M. Parlan, a Pinkerton detective, working from within the Maguires, broke their power. Upon his testimony, between 1877 and 1879 a score of Irishmen were hanged. Historians now think that while some of the leaders were undoubtedly guilty of the crimes for which they were hanged, others were not, but the general atmosphere of hysteria and anti-Irish prejudice prevented fair trials for many. The atrocities of the Maguires have lately come to be viewed not as primitive attempts to organize labor, but rather as textbook illustrations of class warfare and violent rebellion. A parallel may be drawn with black violence of the 1960s. As Frantz Fanon predicted in *The Wretched of the Earth*, "People held in colonial bondage and denied any peaceful avenue to change their estate will resort to violence, indeed almost have to act violently against their tormentors in order to prove their manhood."

Fear of Irish turbulence, their increasing political power, and a new assertiveness on the part of the Roman Catholic Church helped to produce a revival of organized nativism in the late 1880s. Significantly, the American Protective Association, which had absorbed most of the smaller antiforeign and anti-Catholic societies, did not express much interest in the newer immigrants from Southern and Eastern Europe—namely the Italians, Jews, Slavs, Greeks, and Bohemians who were causing so much concern to defenders of "America's Anglo-Saxon purity." Rather, they paid a dubious tribute to the Irish by hurling more abuse at them than at any other nationality. Once again, the Irish hate-literature of earlier nativism began to circulate throughout the country. As was true of similar nativist episodes from the time of the Alien and Sedition Acts of the Federalist era to the Ku Klux Klan of the twentieth century, the A.P.A. fed upon tensions, discontents, fears, and frustrations. Unthinking people acted viscerally, seeking a scapegoat for the problems they could not comprehend. In the nineties, there had been an "agrarian crisis," then the "gold crisis," and finally the "Spanish War crisis." Connected as they were in time, such events enabled the A.P.A. to flourish. When these fears receded in the flush of McKinley prosperity, nativism also evaporated.

In the upper reaches of American society the pattern of discrimination was more durable. In 1922, the Board of Overseers at Harvard College seriously debated establishing a quota of Jewish students. The number of Jews enrolled had increased from seven percent to more than 21 percent, and President A. Lawrence Lowell let it be known that he favored a quota to maintain ethnic balance. But one Harvard man observed: "The Irish, not the Jews present the real problem at Harvard. The new plan of class selection will cut down the number of Irish as well as Jews." Questions on the admission form dealing with religion, and asking whether one's family name had ever been changed would, it was hoped, reduce the number of rough Irish boys who were taking over the leadership in Harvard athletics. The *Boston Transcript* reported, "No religious lines will be drawn but those of Irish descent will be limited." A Harvard undergraduate remarked that only with such restrictions could everyone be sure that all students were of "the right sort." The Irish did not seem to measure up unless they shed their Irishness. Thomas Beer tells the turn-of-the-century story of a lady at a Washington dinner remarking of John McCall, the president of the New York Life Insurance Company. "He's not at all Irish, is he?" McCall asked her sweetly, "Did you expect me to bring a pig and shillelagh with me?" She replied, "Oh dear, no! I don't suppose you even keep a pig, do you?"

In all the larger cities of the country and many of the small towns, the formation of Irish tended to look to their own kind for companionship and recreation. Shrewd and convivial saloonkeepers formed social clubs which lured less shrewd and convivial people together for fellowship. They soon became cogs in the wheels of ward politics. Outrageous working conditions in the mines and factories and sudden reductions in hourly wage scales on the railroads drove Irish workers together. As we have seen, the Ancient Order of Hibernians, at the time a "semisecret" organization, became the formidable influence in miners' unions. Irish militia groups, such as "the Irish Rifles" and the "Napper Tandy Light Artillery," were organized in cities and towns to satisfy the Irish love of ritual and color. The mania in nineteenth century for firefighting was also instrumental in bringing the Irish together, first in volunteer organizations, later in uniformed departments. Al Smith, the unsuccessful Catholic presidential candidate in 1928, developed his love of politics partially through association with and admiration of his uncle, a New York City fireman.

Similarly, the status found in police departments attracted the Irish temperament. By 1933, over 30 percent of the New York City police were Irish or of Irish extraction. It is a truism to equate the Boston or New York policeman with a jovial but short-tempered, brogueish Irishman whose friendship earns him an occasional apple from the neighborhood fruitstand vendor. Chicago Police Commissioner Timothy O'Connor explained why so many Irish joined the force: "The one thing that every man that was a migrant craved was security. Security in his mind existed in two ways—the ownership of property or a Civil Service position. So they became either firemen, policemen, mailmen, or entered some other branch of government or municipal service." Moreover, Irish policemen served as an ideal buffer between old and new Americans. As Thomas J. Fleming noted, they came from a nation where discriminatory English laws were held in small respect and Irish cops could easily make distinctions between "good and bad laws" that the average German or Scandinavian would have found difficult if not impossible to make.

The cultural history of the Irish immigrant began in these groupings and was expressed in his songs, usually melodious, often melancholy; he sang of the land or girl he had left behind him:

> No more among the sycamores
> I'll hear the blackbird sing;
> No more to me the blithe cuckoo
> Will welcome back the spring.

or as in "Kathleen Mavourneen," Al Smith's favorite song:

> Have you forgotten, today we must sever?
> Have you forgotten, today we must part?
> It may be for years, and it may be for ever—
> Then why are you silent, thou voice of my heart?

The most popular singer for the Irish who were fortunate enough to own a hand-crank phonograph was John McCormack, one of the finest *bel canto* voices of the early twentieth century. Irish by birth, he gave concerts throughout the country, mixing a classical repertoire with a few cherished ballads. His recordings of "Macushla," "Kathleen Mavourneen," and "Somewhere a Voice Is Calling" are masterful and definitive.

Irish playwrights are noted for their wit: Oliver Goldsmith, Richard Brinsley Sheridan, Oscar Wilde, George Bernard Shaw, John Millington Synge, and Sean O'Casey rank with the world's best. Works of such literary dramatists were not, however, popular among Irish-Americans. Most of them, authentically American in their tastes, delighted in the idols of the crowd, cheering the exploits of the heavyweight world champions John L. Sullivan and James L. Corbett, and Hall-of-Fame ballplayers Hugh Duffy, Eddie Collins, "Slide" Kelly, "Iron Man" McGinnity, John "Muggsy" McGraw, Cornelius "Connie Mack" McGillicuddy, and Roger Bresnahan, "The Duke of Tralee." For their theatre, "shanty" Irish confined their taste to amateur entertainments, often sponsored by the local firemen's association. "Lace curtain," or *nouveau riche,* Irish preferred the melodrama of Dion Boucicault or John Brougham, two of the most prolific Irish dramatists of the nineteenth century, or the sketches of Irish life in the United States by Harrington and Hart.

Durable stock settings were usually used: a barbershop, a grocery store, or a butcher shop. Unlike the unfavorable stage portrayal of earlier years, when the Irishman had been depicted as a red-nosed, shillelagh-brandishing, vituperative boor, now the Irish characters invariably bested their "straight" men: German or Italian immigrant types became the foils for displays of Irish wit:

So this young Irish lad emigrates to America, attracted by stories of money to be found in the streets. Just after landin' at the dock, he finds a piece of tin in the street, thinkin' it to be a coin. Into a saloon he saunters and says to the barkeep: "Give me a beer." After draining his glass, he puts the tin upon the bar. When the barkeep says, "Dattsa tin!" he replies, "Oh, I beg yer pardon, me good man, I thought it was five!"

Those who lived in large cities enjoyed vaudeville acts like Pat Rooney, the softshoe dancer; Gallagher and Sheen, comedy and song partners; and the operettas of Victor Herbert or of George M. Cohan, who is remembered for his patriotic songs. He wrote "Yankee Doodle Dandy," "It's a Grand Old Flag," and sent America off to the First World War singing "Over There." He also wrote many light musicals and plays such as *Little Nellie Kelly, Forty-Five Minutes from Broadway,* and *The Talk of New York.*

Serious American drama came of age with the premiere of Eugene O'Neill's plays. A handful of his works are considered masterpieces of modern drama: *The Emperor Jones, The Hairy Ape, Desire under the Elms, The Iceman Cometh,* and, published after his death, the autobiographical *Long Day's Journey into Night.* O'Neill was awarded the Nobel Prize for literature in 1936.

Born in New York in 1888, the son of an Irish immigrant, James O'Neill, and Connecticut-born Mary Quinlan, O'Neill spent his early years traveling with his parents throughout the country. His father had given up a budding career as a Shakespearean actor for the security of the title role in a highly successful melodrama, *The Count of Monte Cristo.* While attending a private school in New York, Eugene discovered that his mother had become a drug addict, a habit she had begun years earlier to relieve recovery pains following O'Neill's birth. After praying unsuccessfully that she be released from her addiction, he forsook his Catholicism, although he was, subsequently, haunted by his retreat from religion. One of his plays, *Days without End* (1933), was produced shortly after his brief return to Catholicism. Throughout his life he was often heard to quote a poem that he felt had great personal significance for him: *The Hound of Heaven.* Written by Francis Thompson, the poem concerns a man's flight from God:

> I fled Him, down the nights and down the days;
> I fled Him, down the arches of the years. . . .

O'Neill entered Princeton in 1906, but left the next spring. Abandoning his first wife a few days after he had willfully married her, O'Neill began a career as a merchant seaman, subsequently descending into the limbo of flophouse life in New York City. His health finally broke, and he entered a Connecticut sanatorium, which not only saved his life but marked the beginning of his interest in playwriting. He enrolled in a special drama course at Harvard, and after a year there he returned to New York. O'Neill first won recognition for the one-act plays he wrote for the Provincetown Players, a wharf theatre group on Cape Cod. Success there led to brief winter productions in New York and, in 1920, the production of a full-length play, *Beyond the Horizon,* which won the Pulitzer Prize.

O'Neill was extremely proud that Sean O'Casey, the Irish dramatist, had once assured him, "You write like an Irishman, you don't write like an American." Nearly all his plays reveal his deep Irishness, and in one, *A Moon for the Misbegotten,* he insisted that the entire cast be of Irish ancestry.

Eugene O'Neill's career was highly productive and original. He brought to the American stage a seriousness of themes: the American and Irish-American lust for power and money, the illusions or "pipe dreams" men create to help them face reality, the suffering that men and women inflict on each other because of human frailty. He attempted more than any other American playwright had previously tried: to put tragedy into the American theatre. The relationship between his own personal suffering and that of his characters is one of the major concerns of his biographers.

F. Scott Fitzgerald was the first writer of Irish-Catholic background to become a major novelist in America. Fitzgerald was not a practicing Catholic, perhaps because he viewed the Church as being a particularly unfashionable, Irish-dominated institution. By dropping his Catholicism he also freed himself, he thought, from his Irishness. He was wrong in both instances. His early upbringing as a Catholic accounts for his "habitual" convictions about evil and its effects. Arthur Mizener in his biography of Fitzgerald, *The Far Side of Paradise,* suggests that "it takes a sense of sin which lies far deeper than any nominal commitment to a doctrine to be as powerfully affected by immoral conduct as Fitzgerald was."

In contrast to Irish writers who preceded him, Fitzgerald's Irishness is found in his writing in more intrinsic but less simple ways. Malcolm Cowley in his book *The Literary Situation* contrasts Finley Peter Dunne and Fitzgerald: "Both had been accepted into the ruling Protestant class, but unlike Dunne, who wrote about the Irish, Fitzgerald wrote about the Protestant group. Therefore, although his Irishness is a little *disguised,* it remains an incentive in all his stories; it gave him a sense of standing apart that sharpened his observation of social differences."

Edmund Wilson, a friend and Princeton classmate of Fitzgerald's, underscored this duality in an article in 1922, later reprinted in his *Shores of Light* (1952):

In regard to the man himself, there are perhaps two things worth knowing, for the influence they have had on his work. In the first place, he comes from the Middle West. . . . The second thing one should know about him is that Fitzgerald is partly Irish and that he brings both to life and fiction certain qualities that are not Anglo-Saxon. For, like the Irish, Fitzgerald is romantic, but also cynical about romance; he is bitter as well as ecstatic; astringent as well as lyrical. He casts himself in the role of playboy, yet as the playboy he incessantly mocks. He is vain, a little malicious, of quick intelligence and wit, and has an Irish gift for turning language into something iridescent and surprising.

Malcolm Cowley and William V. Shannon have also emphasized that an appreciation of Fitzgerald's Irish heritage is basic to understanding his fiction, while Leslie Fiedler in *An End to Innocence* argues persuasively that the Irish-ness of Fitzgerald's characters reveals both the external sophistication for which Fitzgerald strived, and his genuine personality (behind the author's interposed mask). The very Irishness of the character is always a clue, maintains Fiedler. Of *Tender Is the Night,* he writes, "Almost all the main characters, whatever their outsides, turn out to be F. Scott Fitzgerald. Dick Diver, the protagonist, who seems from a distance the assured aristocrat, the obverse of the author, reveals on the first close-up the Irish lilt, the drunkenness, the tortured sensibility that are Fitzgerald's."

It is not surprising to find a lace-curtain Irishman stepping into a Protestant world of wealth and luxury drawing upon a double view of himself. Fitzgerald was both actor and spectator in life; he had the romantic weakness to pursue the moment recklessly, but he also had the inbred morality of his early training, and his sense of the incongruous to remind him not to take his posture that seriously.

Everything implicit in Fitzgerald's work which reveals his desire to lose his lace-curtain Irish past is more explicit and more pronounced in the writing of John O'Hara. Born in Pottsville, Pennsylvania, the son of a doctor and the first of eight children, O'Hara sensed early in life that his father's position and income separated him from the hardy Irish and Polish youngsters on the wrong side of the tracks. But what bothered him was the low status of his comparatively well-to-do Catholicism when measured against the world of the wealthy Protestants a few blocks up the avenue. Pottsville was to become the "Gibbs-ville" of his novels and he concerned himself with the life style of the cardboard, lacquered, Protestant establishment he so admired. O'Hara produced a number of popular and financially successful works: *Appointment in Samarra, Butterfield 8, A Rage to Live, Ten North Frederick, From the Terrace* and *Ourselves to Know.* But his work failed to receive the critical recognition he openly longed for partly because he had excised his Irish heritage. His writing is devoid of the passion of life, of a reality which seizes the reader because of its truth.

At the risk of oversimplification, it may be argued that O'Hara evaded his true subject—the conflict between his aspirations and an insecurity deriving from his lack of the right education, nationality, and religion. Thus, we have the unusual picture of a discontented Irishman writing about what he would like to be—an established Protestant. Instead of capturing the torment of the Irish outsider struggling against what he once called his "peasant status," Catholicism, or showing us the nature, quality, or causes for unarticulated hopes, we have characters with cool manners and postures. We read O'Hara and we keep hoping that he is using restrained and brilliant satire in depicting the fallowness of a segment of society we do not know. Perhaps he is. Yet somehow we are left finally with a strange uneasy impression that what O'Hara is showing us is what he wanted for himself.

Another important Irish-American novelist is James T. Farrell, the most effective of the left-wing naturalists of the era of the Great Depression. Applying the tenets of naturalism to his working-class Irish Catholic background,

Farrell produced the *Studs Lonigan* trilogy. Alfred Kazin suggests that Farrell remembered nothing and learned from nothing but his youth. But that was enough:

Unlike all the little people in left-wing letters who loved the working-class to death but could never touch them, Farrell was joined by every instinct to men and women who have claimed the earth to live from one day to the next. What more was needed in Studs Lonigan than the literal transcription of the Irish Babbittry's inhuman yammering, with abysmal cruelty banging against animal insolence, where only Celtic blood could get back at Celts with so much grisly humor?

Farrell's hero, or more precisely, as current literary jargon has it, "nonhero," Studs Lonigan, represents Farrell's indictment of the American Irishmen's church, school, and home. Farrell's chief objections to the cultural impoverishment of Irish Catholicism are shown in Studs' failure to be touched by them. He has little motivation other than to someday become successful, or, as the Irish put it, to "get ahead"; the boy's imaginative impulses receive no encouragement, so by the time he enters his teens he has substituted the values of the streetcorner Napoleons and the poolroom Platos to fill the void. Discussing Studs Lonigan's uniqueness, John Chamberlain points out: "He wants to be a big shot, to have style, to achieve a romantic personal identity. The streets and the boyhood gang capture this adventurousness and imagination and provide him with his only ideal." But Studs himself expresses his ideal in much simpler phrasing. He wants, as he puts it, "to be strong, and tough, and the real stuff." Studs' "real stuff" accomplishments in life are cracked hopes, alcoholic frustrations, economic mediocrity, a joyless, stolid marriage, and in the last hours of his life the ignominy of a needless death.

Hunger, dissatisfaction, provocation, and ambition brought the Irish immigrants to our shores. Their legacy to America is in the work of their hands and backs. Their desire to make progress was transmitted to their sons, many of whom, deprived of a rich cultural heritage because of their parents' own limited opportunities, nevertheless improved their own stations through their talent and industry. They became office workers, civil servants, and professionals, people whose cautious security was abetted by their loyal Catholicism. But the Irish-American writer had a larger dream. No mere security or servile clock-watching for him. The American ideal he sought was one of grace, leisure, wealth, travel—a world ruled by the Anglo-Saxon aristocracy of finance and commerce.

Here was where the poetry of life lay, not in another rung up on the Irish Catholic ladder. O'Neill, Farrell, Fitzgerald, and O'Hara felt this gap because they were artists and Irish. They put aside their Catholicism, viewing it as regressive, complacent, and a social and cultural hindrance. In effect, they were also hoping thereby to cast off the albatross of their Irishness. These writers, like most writers who are Irish—James Joyce, William Butler Yeats, and Sean O'Casey—were autobiographical in their fiction. But perhaps because of early training they have been in addition *moral.* The pervasive sense of guilt found in O'Neill's characters may be partially explained by his flight from the religion of his ancestry. Farrell wrote of the impoverishment of Catholicism, using Studs Lonigan as a mythic example of what happened to others and could have happened to him. Fitzgerald and O'Hara entered the realm they sought, and they recorded what they saw. Both exposed it, but perhaps Fitzgerald came to closer grips in his fiction with the dual life he led as both defendant and judge than O'Hara came by his cataloguing of the careless life at the top.

In the areas of popular culture also, the Irish have received recognition for their achievements. Movies have made celebrities of Bing Crosby, Gene Kelly, Pat O'Brien, James Cagney, Maureen O'Hara, Grace Kelly, and the Barrymore family—Ethel, Lionel, and John, the last-named being one of the most renowned Shakespearean actors America has yet produced—while John Huston and John Ford have won acclaim as two of the finest directors in American film.

In a perceptive study of social discrimination against the Irish, Thomas N. Brown saw the decades from 1870 to 1900 as a period of slow advancement, a kind of plateau sloping upward. After 1900, the ascent was more precipitous, and the Irish firmly established themselves in the middle class. Evidence of this new status can be found in the proliferation of Catholic educational institutions of higher learning, in the classification of the Irish by racial purists of the age as one of the "superior" Nordic peoples, and in the large numbers of successful Irish businessmen slavishly copying the business methods of the Yankees with whom they worked.

In truth, it seems safe to say that the Irish purchased acceptance by paying the price of conformity. They got along when they accepted the traditional American values of work, progress, success, and respectability. When they organized labor unions or lobbied for Irish freedom, then people talked about "the Irish problem." One is tempted to argue that whenever they did anything original or freewheeling, they could expect opposition. Certainly, other Americans resented the Irish political style, and in politics, where their role was not imitative but truly creative, the Irish have left perhaps their most lasting impression on American life.

Sources

Beer, Thomas, *The Mauve Decade,* New York, 1926.

Broehl, Wayne G., *The Molly Maguires,* Cambridge, Mass., 1964.

Brown, Thomas N., "Social Discrimination against the Irish in the United States" (pamphlet), American Jewish Committee, November 1968.

Cohan, George M., *Twenty Years on Broadway,* New York, 1925.

Cowley, Malcolm, *The Literary Situation,* New York, 1958.

Ellis, Elmer, *Mr. Dooley's America,* New York, 1941.

Farrell, James T., *Studs Lonigan,* New York, 1938.

Fiedler, Leslie, *An End to Innocence,* Boston, 1955.

Fitzgerald, F. Scott, *The Great Gatsby,* New York, 1925.

Fleming, Thomas J., "The Policeman's Lot," *American Heritage,* Vol. XXI, No. 2, February 1970.

Ford, Corey, *Donovan of Oss,* Boston, 1970.

Gelb, Arthur and Dorothy, *O'Neill,* New York, 1965.

Headley, Joel Tyler, *The Great Riots of New York 1712–1873,* Indianapolis, 1970. (First published 1873.)

Higham, John, *Strangers in the Land: Patterns of American Nativism, 1860–1925,* New Brunswick, N. J., 1955.

Kazin, Alfred, *On Native Ground,* New York, 1956.

Mann, Arthur, *Yankee Reformers in the Urban Age,* Cambridge, Mass., 1954.

Mizener, Arthur, *The Far Side of Paradise,* Boston, 1951.

Nevins, Allan, and Milton H. Thomas, Editors, *The Diary of George Templeton Strong,* New York, 1952.

Olmstead, Frederick Law, *A Journey in the Seaboard Slave States in the Years 1853–1854,* New York, 1904.

Reynolds, Robert L., "The Coal Kings Come to Judgment," *American Heritage,* Vol. XI, No. 3, April 1960.

Schlesinger, Arthur M., Jr., *A Pilgrim's Progress: Orestes A. Brownson,* Boston, 1966.

Solomon, Barbara, *Ancestors and Immigrants: A Changing New England Tradition,* Cambridge, Mass., 1956.

Turnbull, Andrew, *Scott Fitzgerald,* New York, 1962.

Wilson, Edmund, *Shores of Light,* New York, 1952.

Chapter Five

Politics: Irish Style

In a word association game, the word "Irish" may provoke a single rejoinder: "politician." Irish and politics have gone together throughout American history. As early as Washington's administration, Federalist politicians were complaining of "wild Irish" flocking into the country and supporting the Jeffersonian Republicans. A hundred years later an observer noted that "one of the functions of the Irish race in America is to administer the affairs of American cities." He found at least 17 cities scattered across the country among those "led captive by Irishmen and their sons."

The era so described was the heyday of Irish political power. Although this power has declined perceptibly since then, it has by no means vanished. Another writer has called the administration of John F. Kennedy "the last hurrah" for the Irish-Americans, because on the day he died the President of the United States, the Speaker of the House of Representatives, the Majority Leader of the United States Senate, and the Chairman of the Democratic National Committee were all Irish-Catholic Democrats. By 1968, however, when two Irish-American Senators, Robert F. Kennedy and Eugene McCarthy, contested for the Democratic presidential nomination, talk of the last hurrah seemed premature.

How does one account for the remarkable political accomplishments of the Irish-Americans? A good place to look for clues is in their history. Certain features of the Irish experience stand out. First of all, as we have seen, Irish immigrants tended to live in large cities, making it easier for their leaders to form them into cohesive voting blocs. The poverty of the earliest immigrants made them highly conscious of their community of interests. Mass voting in cities such as New York, Philadelphia, Boston, and Chicago not only led to control of municipal governments, but affected state and, ultimately, national policy. However, density of population cannot singly explain the Irish political phenomenon, because later immigrant peoples also huddled together by hundreds of thousands in urban ghettos failed to follow the Irish pattern. The difference is that, unlike the other newcomers, the Irish spoke English. Irish Nationalists would later deplore the replacement of Gaelic by English as the language of the Irish peasantry, but to the future emigrants it proved an invaluable advantage.

Moreover, among the immigrant peoples, the Irish alone comprehended the essentials of Anglo-Saxon democracy. In Ireland, they had understood the form of representative government, although they had not been allowed to participate in its function. They could appreciate the significance and power of such offices as sheriff, surrogate, alderman, and mayor. Usually, peasants emigrated from Europe with real distrust or fear of government, and more than likely a family's last encounter with officials had been an unhappy one, given the bureaucratic obstacles those departing usually had to overcome. The Irish, on the other hand, saw in politics the possibilities for a profession offering social status and economic security.

Above and beyond these considerations (which may be described as environmental factors), there remain the intangible reasons, chiefly the aggressiveness, the conviviality, the wit, the organizational "know-how" so often associated with Irish-American politicians. Such qualities are unique to the American experience; even Irishmen visiting the United States were as impressed as native Americans by Irish-American political acumen. Historians are currently on unpopular ground when they attribute supposed traits to certain ethnic groups, but a relish for the mechanics of politics and a flair for its practice conspire to explain the persistence of Celtic success generations after environmental explanations are no longer relevant.

Traditionally, Irish politics operated within the framework of the Democratic Party. Attracted to the infant Jeffersonian party by its antiauthoritarian philosophy and its distrust of England, they found themselves welcomed and cultivated. Their identification with the Democrat-Republicans increased in the wake of emotional—indeed, almost irrational—attacks on the Irish by leaders of the Federalist Party, to whom they were doubly suspect: First, the Federalists abhorred their revolutionary tendencies. Had not the abortive United Irishmen rebellion of 1798 drawn its inspiration and substantial support from the radical Jacobins in France? Irish revolutionaries such as Wolfe Tone and Napper Tandy sought exile in the United States, thereby confirming the worst fears of the New England Federalist Harrison Gray Otis, who "did not wish to invite hordes of Wild Irishmen, nor the turbulent and disorderly of all parts of the world, to come here with a view to disturb our tranquillity, after having succeeded in the overthrow of their own governments." Worst of all, the Irish, "the most God-provoking democrats this side of Hell," by allying themselves with the Jeffersonians, would insure the eventual demise of Federalism. To prevent the United States from becoming "the vassal of foreign outlaws," the Federalists enacted the infamous Alien and Sedition Acts. Debates in Congress and in the press over the Naturalization Act contain many references to the "Irish menace." Federalist rhetoric abounds with "agents of the French Revolution in disguise," "malignant forces of disorder," and "excesses of Democracy." A provision lengthening the residence requirement for citizenship failed to satisfy the more extreme nativists actually favoring that *citizenship be restricted to the native-born.* Disenfranchising the immigrant would serve a dual purpose by promoting domestic tranquillity and depriving Jefferson of many votes.

Not surprisingly, the Irish reacted angrily to the anti-immigrant bias of the Alien Acts and to the repressiveness of the Sedition acts. The first person convicted under the latter was Matthew Lyon (dubbed "Spitting Lyon," since he had once spat upon a Federalist in the House of Representatives), an Irish-born editor and congressman from Vermont, who had printed a letter recommending that the Federalist President, John Adams, be committed to a mad-house. With his arrest, Lyon became a martyr-hero to the Irish, and the Jeffersonians were handed a potent issue for the presidential campaign of 1800. After Jefferson's victory, Congress repealed the detested legislation, and the Irish were confirmed in their devotion to the Democratic-Republicans. In a sense, this development was ironic, because few of the Irish immigrants really harbored revolutionary tendencies. Better handling by the Federalists might have inveigled some of them from the Jeffersonians. Given the aristocratic and nativist bias of the Federalists, however, any other response to the newcomers may have been impossible. As late as 1812, the party unsuccessfully opposed the extension of the suffrage in New York State for fear of increasing the Irish vote.

As Celtic immigration spurted after 1815, the significance of Irish voting power did also, eventually providing a key element in the triumph of Jacksonian democracy. Historians have disagreed about the nature of that movement and the contradictory personality and controversial policies of "Old Hickory," but his appeal to the Irish was undeniable, apparently from the moment they stepped off the boats. Charles Latrobe, an English poet and one of the many foreign visitors to America during the 1830s, described the arrival of an immigrant ship:

Here comes a shipload of Irish. They land upon the wharfs of New York in rags and open-knee'd-breeches, with raw looks and bare necks. They flourish their cudgels, throw up their torn hats, and cry, "Hurrah for Gineral Jackson!"

Such affection came naturally because Irish ideas on politics (on almost everything really) continued to be colored by anti-English feeling, and the Hero of New Orleans, whose parents had emigrated to America from the North of Ireland two years before his birth, was famous for his Anglophobia. Jacksonian politicos welcomed the Irish, met them at the docks, eased their naturalization difficulties, enrolled them in the Democratic Party, and eventually nominated them for offices. Their solicitous concern contrasted sharply with the standoffish attitude of Jackson's chief opponents, the Whigs.

To the Irish, the Whig Party, consisting largely of men of property and imbued with nativist prejudice, was a lineal descendant of the Federalist. A strong streak of abolitionism among Northern Whigs also offended the immigrant, who saw the black man as a competitor in the cheap labor markets. In most states, the Whig leadership wrote off the Irish as hopelessly Democratic, but some of the more perceptive leaders realized the folly of alienating an ever-growing segment of the electorate. In New York, where the foreign-born held the balance of power as early as 1840, Whig leaders William H. Seward and Thurlow Weed enjoyed some success in wooing the Irish. As governor, Seward received considerable support resulting from his criticism of the Protestant controlled Public School Society and his endorsement of a proposal disbursing public funds to parochial schools.

But Seward's success was almost unique. Except for the small number of Protestant Irish who became Whigs precisely because they sought to shed their identification with the impoverished newcomers, the Irish continued solidly Democratic. In New York State, where Irish Catholics formed the single largest immigrant bloc, 95 percent of their votes went to the Democratic presidential candidate in 1844. Occasional appeals by Whig nominees to the Irish found a cold reception. In 1852, General Winfield Scott, running for the presidency on the Whig ballot, made a sentimental speech at Columbus, Ohio: "I think I hear again that rich brogue that betokens a son of old Ireland. I love to hear it! I heard it on the Niagara in '14 and again in the valley of Mexico. It will always remind me of the gallant men of Erin who in such great numbers have followed me to victory." The Irish-American press reacted skeptically. As one editor expressed it, "Now, at any other time, such a vindication of our countrymen would be most grateful. But larking or sparking with 'that soft Irish brogue' at this moment, immediately before the Presidential Election, has not the grace of modesty or sincerity about it. 'Gineral, Gineral, you are a big deludherer!' "

To the Irishman's way of thinking, the Democrats demonstrated their feelings more concretely by nominating Irishmen for office. In that same election of 1852, 18 Irish-American Democrats were elected in New York State alone.

In the tumultuous national politics of the years before the Civil War, the Irish steadfastly championed the expansionist foreign policy and the conservative domestic posture of the Democratic administrations of Presidents Polk, Pierce, and Buchanan. Enthusiastic backers of Polk in his quarrel with Mexico, they also played a prominent role in the "Young America" movement of the 1850s. One of the most ardent propagandizers of expansion, John L. O'Sullivan, coined the watchword of the era when he wrote in the *Democratic Review* of July 1854 of "our manifest destiny to overspread the continent allotted by Providence for the free development of our yearly mutliplying millions." The tag "manifest destiny," quickly transformed into a doctrine, not only served as an easy rationalization for the annexation of a large part of Mexico in 1848, but would be revived a half century later to justify the acquisition of the Philippine Islands and Puerto Rico after the Spanish-American War.

Irish involvement in the Young America movement did not spring solely from hopes of extending the republic southward into the Caribbean; in addition, it could possibly serve as a vehicle for the encouragement of revolutionary movements abroad, specifically in Ireland. Irish newspapers blazoned the expansionist slogan, "Cuba by Purchase or War," and mass meetings of Irishmen rang with the cries of "William Walker and Nicaragua." But John Mitchel, one of the heroes of the abortive Young Ireland rebellion of 1848, who found exile in New York City after escape from a British penal colony in Tasmania, made it clear that his interest in Young America sprang from a desire to stimulate "the movement of European Democracy and especially of Irish independence." He hoped America could prove the testing ground "prayed for by Archimedes, whereon they may plant a lever that shall move the world."

In the end, it all turned out to be little more than slogans and bombast. Leaders of nations undergoing serious internal turmoil often try to distract the populace through overseas adventures or sword-rattling against foreign enemies, real or imagined. Mao's China in the 1960s affords a recent example of this maneuver. In retrospect, Young America can be interpreted as a device to distract attention from issues related to slavery. These issues proved to be too fundamental, however, to be shunted aside.

Curiously enough, the Know-Nothing phenomenon of the same decade, which many see simply as the political manifestation of a virulent nativism, was *also* an attempt to straddle the slavery question. In this respect, it is instructive as a case study of the classic response to any troublesome issue: scapegoat-hunting. Mere railing against immigrants and Catholics hardly helped find an answer to the problem in the territories, yet the temper of the times caused many to respond to simplistic rant. As noted in the previous chapter, fear, hatred, and jealousy of the Irish attracted the greatest adherents to nativism, but a compact minority joined the "American Party"—a label the Know-Nothings stuck on their political organization—simply because it promised to abstain from wrangling over sectional issues.

For a season, the Know-Nothings enjoyed a considerable success, winning control or a strong voice in a half-dozen legislatures and electing a substantial bloc of congressmen. But the party never possessed any real stability. Even Horace Greeley, whose *New York Tribune* consistently harassed the Irish and occasionally endorsed nativist proposals, sardonically allowed that the Know-Nothings were "as devoid of the elements of persistence as an anti-cholera or anti-potato-rat party would be."

Coming together in national conventions, the Know-Nothings discovered that nativism could not effectually serve as a cloak to cover sectional disagreements. Despite its numbers in Congress, the party made no progress whatsoever in its attempt to extend the naturalization period and otherwise restrict the rights of the foreign-born. Its sole nativist achievement was Senate enactment of a rider to the Kansas-Nebraska Act, excluding recent immigrants from voting in territorial elections. Even this victory proved short-lived: When the bill reached the House of Representatives, the political privileges of the unnaturalized settlers were restored.

Similar setbacks happened in the states, and Massachusetts provides a good example. Here the Know-Nothings gained almost complete power, thanks to support from the state's reform element. Whether they directed their efforts toward abolition, temperance, or school or electoral improvements, the reformers of the Bay State found themselves frustrated by a coalition of conservative businessmen with Southern interests—and the Irish. The nativist legislature did enact a good deal of progressive legislation, including reform of the school system, abolition of imprisonment for debt, and increased power for juries. Its antiforeignism, supposedly its reason for existence, did not amount to much. In fact, the fruitful accomplishments of the legislature were politically negated by outraged public reaction to the shenanigans of "a nunnery investigating committee" which had billed the state for expenses incurred in a visit to a house of prostitution in Lowell.

Meanwhile, thoughtful Americans spoke out against the betrayal of American principles inherent in nativism. Andrew Johnson of Tennessee challenged, "Show me a Know-Nothing and I will show you a reptile on whose neck every foot ought to be placed," while Abraham Lincoln wrote, in 1855, to a friend who had inquired about his political stance:

That is a disputed point. I think I am a whig; but others say there are no whigs, and that I am an abolitionist. . . . I now do no more than oppose the *extension* of slavery. I am not a Know-Nothing. That is certain. How could I be? How can any one who abhors the oppression of negroes, be in favor of degrading classes of white people? Our progress in degeneracy appears to me to be pretty rapid. As a nation, we began by declaring that *"all men are created equal."* We now practically read it "all men are created equal, *except negroes.*" When the Know-Nothings get control, it will read "all men are created equal, except negroes, *and foreigners, and catholics.*" When it comes to this I should prefer emigrating to some country where they make no pretense of loving liberty—to Russia, for instance, where despotism can be taken pure, and without the base alloy of hypocracy [sic].

The American Party, running ex-President Millard Fillmore as its presidential candidate in 1856, managed to obtain 25 percent of the popular vote, but by 1860 the political force of nativism had been spent. For the Irish, the net effect of the episode had been to cement their ties to the Democrats. The Republican Party, which had emerged from the confusion attending the passage of the Kansas-Nebraska Act and the demise of the Whig Party, received scant support from them, for Republicanism seemed nothing more than "old Whiggery writ large," and the abolitionist coloring of the new party together with its attractiveness to nativist and temperance elements increased their antipathy. Of course, when the Civil War came, the Irish proved their willingness to fight and die for the country that meant so much to them, but unlike many other Northerners they simply did not equate defense of the Union with espousal of the Republican Party. After the war, they questioned the wisdom of the Republican plan for reconstructing the South, backed Andrew Johnson in his struggle with the Radicals, and disregarded appeals to vote for their old commander, General Grant, in 1868 and 1872.

William Marcy "Boss" Tweed, the last old-stock American to serve as a leader of Tammany Hall, the essentially extra-legal organization that functioned as the regular Democratic Party in New York, was sent to jail in 1873, and "Honest John" Kelly succeeded him as boss of Tammany. Kelly's assumption of power marks the beginning of the age of Irish-dominated urban political machines. The Boss System began in New York, but soon spread to almost every fairly large city in America, in such manner at times that it seemed the political machine was a natural, almost essential phenomenon in the growth of the cities. Not all the bosses were Irish. But a majority of them were, and in New York, which started the style with Kelly, Irishmen were to ride the "Tammany Tiger," for fifty years.

Curiously enough, the Society of the Sons of Tammany, founded in 1783 to uphold the ideals of democracy in its early years, had been somewhat less than enthusiastic about the influx of poor Irish immigrants into New York. Members of the society opposed any relaxation of their original prohibition against "full" membership for the foreign-born, and such reluctance did not disappear until angry Irishmen took matters into their own hands and almost demolished the Tammany Wigwam (headquarters) during an uproarious melee in April 1817.

Afterwards, the Hibernian influence steadily increased. The enfranchisement of the propertyless (the New York State constitution of 1822 ordained universal manhood suffrage) at once insured the growth of Tammany's political power and gave the Irish a rightful voice in the exercise of that power. Through the years, the Grand Sachems recognized the Irish with nominations for Congress, the State Senate and Assembly, and lesser state offices, but with Kelly, the Irish began *distributing* the patronage.

Kelly's tenure as Tammany leader did more than symbolize the arrival of the Irish at the summit, because "Honest John" made a lasting and significant contribution to American politics. Kelly transformed Tammany Hall into an organization operating with an efficiency that not Tweed nor any of his other predecessors ever imagined. In the words of one admirer, Kelly found Tammany "a horde" and left it "an army." He accomplished this change by designing an elaborate hierarchical structure to maintain discipline and order. As the chart that follows illustrates, Tammany built its power upon votes, and the machine retained its effectiveness by catering to the needs of mostly immigrant voters. The machine survived because the block and election-district captains, the assembly-district leaders, and, ultimately, the boss himself worked hard at keeping the voters satisfied.

It was a highly personal business. What mattered to the machine's voter was not what happened in Washington, or even, for that matter, in the state capitals, but what was going on in his neighborhood; more particularly he asked, how could he be helped? Perhaps a father had lost a job, a son had run afoul of the law, a daughter's husband drank too much. Could the block captain help? Would the new firehouse in Ward Eight mean more jobs for the residents? Did the city plan to build a new park on Tenth Street?

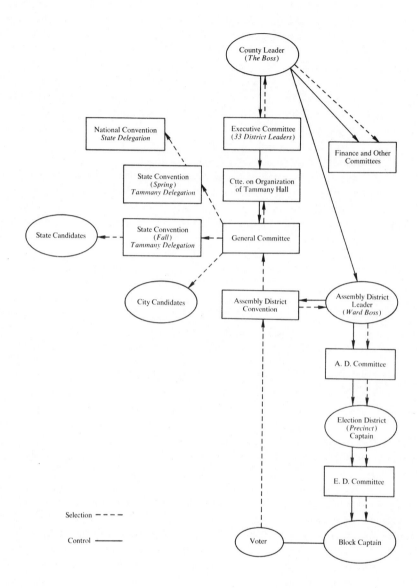

Honest John's Tammany Hall*

Reformers who periodically tried to throw out the political machines found the immigrant voter puzzling to understand. There was a strange willingness of the newcomers to condone corruption for the sake of minor favors; as one reformer complained, the immigrant lacked the faculty of abstraction, and thought not of the welfare of the community, but only of himself. But Oscar Handlin has perceptively remarked, "It never occurred to this critic that precious little thought was given by others to the welfare of the newcomers. If they did not consider their own interests, no one else would."

George Washington Plunkitt, a Tammany district leader for almost fifty years, credited his endurance to being on the spot when help was needed:

If a family is burned out, I don't ask whether they are Republicans or Democrats, and I don't refer them to the Charity Organization Service which would investigate their case in a month or two and decide they were worthy of help about the time they are dead from starvation. I just get quarters for them, buy clothes for them if their clothes were burned up, and fix them up till they got things runnin' again. It's philanthropy but it's politics—mighty good politics. Who can tell how many votes one of these fires bring me?

Plunkitt and countless other leaders in cities across the nation dealt in tangibles: food, jobs, a scuttle of coal in the winter, excursions in the summer. Against these, the reformer thumped on civil service reform, economy in government, and more efficient administration of the laws, promising to reduce property taxes and to curtail public services. Not surprisingly, they terrified the immigrant voter. Economy in government and reduction of taxes often translated into loss of desperately needed jobs in municipal police, fire, or sanitation departments! And what did a program of efficient administration of the laws mean to the immigrant? Too often only trouble. As Finley Peter Dunne's famous newspaper creation, Mr. Dooley, the loquacious saloonkeeper of Archey Road, put it:

Th' woman nex' dure is locked up f'r sthringin' a clothesline on th' roof, Hannigan's boy Tim gets tin days f'r keeping a goat, th' polis reserves are called out to protict the vested right iv property against th' haynyous pushcart man, th' stations is crowded with felons charged with maintainin' a hose conthrary to th' statchoos made an' provided, an' th' tenderline is all over twon. A rayformer doesn't think anything has been accomplished if they'se a vacan bedroom in the pinitenchry. His motto is "Arrest that man."

So the middle-class reformers made little headway; the immigrant bloc remained loyal to the machines. By providing the ghetto poor with a badly needed stake in society, a chance to participate in the American dream of getting ahead, the boss gave much for asking little, as newcomers saw it. Finally, the Irish shared with other immigrants an instinctive dislike of reformers, because the latter were usually drawn from the better, Protestant elements of the cities. In Boston, for example, the Brahmin leaders did not bother to conceal their contempt for the Celts; they apparently found it impossible not to be patronizing. Thus Edward Everett Hale urged the Protestant churches to open neighborhood centers in Irish areas in order "to teach the Irishmen why his race has been kept down and by what sure teaching it shall rise." Sentiments such as these caused the Boston poet and editor John Boyle O'Reilly to arraign the arrogant do-gooders for their

> Organized charity, scrimped and iced
> In the name of a cautious, statistical Christ.

All that was asked in return, by the machine, was a vote. Contrary to popular legend, little outright buying of votes was used. It was unnecessary; everywhere the Irishman went—to his job, to his saloon, to his church—reminders of the organization's influence abounded. It should be noted, however, as several recent studies have shown, that the immigrant voter was ready to vote against the declared position of the boss when he thought it in his wisest interest to do so.

For the boss to hand out jobs, to supply baskets of food, to have a persuasive influence with the forces of justice, required money. He obtained money by doing favors. For a consideration, it was possible to obtain a license for a saloon or to have one denied to a competitor. If the regulations of the municipal street department proved too onerous for operators of street railways, the boss could see to it they became more "reasonable." Opportunities for corruption were almost limitless, because the rapid growth of cities required large-scale expansion of public utilities; and businessmen with lax consciences competed with each other for lucrative contracts or franchises to build waterworks, lay trolley tracks, construct public buildings, or dispose of garbage. One source had calculated that Boss McMann of Philadelphia had over 5600 jobs at his disposal and received annually from each officeholder a stated percentage of his yearly salary. He left an estate valued at over two million dollars.

In addition, there were more disreputable sources of income for the machines: Payoffs were forthcoming if officials tacitly permitted gambling houses and prostitution dens; and, of course, at times downright stealing of public funds took place. Most of the later bosses avoided the mistakes of the notorious Tweed Ring, which had openly plundered New York City of millions. They preferred "honest graft." What did this apparent contradiction mean? Again, we can turn to the inimitable George Washington Plunkitt for an explanation.

Everybody is talkin' these days about Tammany men growin' rich on graft, but nobody thinks of drawin' the distinction between honest graft and dishonest graft. There's all the difference in the world between the two. Yes, many of our men have grown rich in politics. I have myself. I've made a big fortune out of the game, and I'm gettin' richer every day, but I've not gone in for dishonest graft—blackmailin' gamblers, saloon-keepers, disorderly people, etc.—and neither has any of the men who have made big fortunes in politics.

There's an honest graft, and I'm an example of how it works. I might sum up the whole thing by sayin': "I seen my opportunities and I took 'em."

Just let me explain by examples. My party's in power in the city, and it's goin' to undertake a lot of public improvements. Well, I'm tipped off, say, that they're going to lay out a new park at a certain place.

I see my opportunity and I take it. I go to that place and I buy up all the land I can in the neighborhood. Then the board of this or that makes its plan public, and there is a rush to get my land, which nobody cared particular for before.

Ain't it perfectly honest to charge a good price and make a profit on my investment and foresight? Of course, it is. Well, that's honest graft.

The relative political sophistication, cohesiveness, and awareness of the Irish-Americans (contrasted with other immigrant peoples), coupled with their concentration in key states, made them a pivotal factor in the closely contested presidential elections of the post-Civil War era. The endorsement of Irish independence by both national parties provides one good indicator of the attention paid to the Irish voter. Though space does not permit an extended discussion of the Irish role in national elections, two examples will help to illuminate it. In 1884, the Republicans clearly made a determined effort to attract Irish support inasmuch as their candidate, James G. Blaine, had a built-in appeal. Of Irish descent, with a Roman Catholic mother and a cousin a nun, Blaine had gratified Irish nationalists through his calculated Anglophobia during a short stint as Secretary of State. In addition to being firmly on record for a free Ireland, Blaine had even termed his support of the high protective tariff as an attempt to protect America from the pro-British, free-trade devices of the Democrats.

A number of Irish leaders quickly organized a campaign in behalf of the G.O.P. standard bearer. John Devoy's *Irish Nation* and Patrick Ford's *Irish World,* two of the country's most influential Celtic newspapers, both vigorously endorsed Blaine. Great rallies were held for him in New York; and in Boston a convention of the Irish Land League, carried away by its own exuberance, proclaimed that Blaine's election would mean the freedom of Ireland within thirty days!

National Democratic leaders did not hide their concern over a possible mass defection of the Irish. The situation in New York seemed particularly bad. Relations between Honest John Kelly's Tammany Hall and New York State's governor Grover Cleveland, the Democratic Presidential candidate, never cordial, had deteriorated to the point where some feared Tammany leaders might make public their disaffection from the Democrats by recommending a vote for the candidate of the Greenback Party, Benjamin F. Butler. Everyone realized the importance of New York's 36 electoral votes in what was expected to be a very close election.

In late October, Blaine carried his campaign to New York City. He agreed to meet with a large delegation of Protestant ministers. The honor of delivering the main speech at the gathering was given to the city's oldest parson, the Rev. Samuel D. Burchard. Although Burchard had a reputation as a fiery nativist, no one expected him to raise the sensitive religious issue at a political meeting. But he did, producing the most memorable American political phrase since "Tippecanoe and Tyler, too." "We are Republicans," declared Dr. Burchard, "and don't propose to leave our party to identify ourselves with the party whose antecedents have been rum, Romanism and Rebellion."

In one sentence, an anathema had been hurled at Southerners, antiprohibitionists, and Catholics. Most of all, however, it seemed a direct hit at the religion, drinking habits, and loyalty of the Irish. Senator Arthur Gorman of Maryland, manager of the campaign of the Democratic candidate Grover Cleveland, realized at once the impact of the incident. Learning that Blaine had failed to repudiate Burchard's remarks, he instructed, "This sentence must be in every daily newspaper in the country tomorrow, no matter how, no matter what it costs . . . and it must be kept alive for the rest of the campaign."

Blaine moved to disassociate himself from Burchard, but too late. Cleveland carried New York with a plurality of 1149 votes out of over 1,167,000 cast. While Cleveland's vote declined about 70 percent in Irish wards in New York City and Boston from that of the Democratic candidate in 1880, Blaine had probably lost enough Irish votes by Burchard's unfortunate alliteration to cost him the state, and, as expected, the loss of New York proved decisive.

Four years later both parties again competed strongly for the endorsement of the Irish-American voter. The Democrats circulated stories that Benjamin Harrison, the Republican nominee, had slurred the Irish, calling them fit only to dig ditches. For their part, the Republicans used a naturalized American citizen of English birth named Murchison to extract an incredibly stupid letter from the British minister in Washington, Lord Sackville-West, favoring the re-election of Grover Cleveland. It was now the Republicans' turn to spread propaganda; the Irish and the Murchison letter may well have made the difference in New York, a victory Harrison won by some 13,000 votes. Throughout the nation, Cleveland had a popular plurality of over 100,000 votes, but the unrepresentative electoral system gave him 168 electoral votes to 233 for his opponent. With a change in New York, he would have had 204 votes and Harrison 197.

Along with other immigrant groups, the Irish are often considered to have a conservative rather than a liberal influence on politics, although Americans who expressed misgivings over the hordes of newcomers pouring into the country at the turn of the century often charged the immigrant with radical politics. The peasant origin of so many of the immigrants, the backwardness of their old societies, their desire to hold onto as much as possible of the old heritage, the strong emphasis of their churches (especially the views of the Catholic Church on the need for submissiveness to authority), tended to make them generally conservative.

But this generalization, while perhaps true enough for most ethnic groups, is not entirely so when applied to the Irish. For one thing, although the urban Irish did not flock in large numbers to the socialist movement, they did produce a significant number of leaders in radical politics. A conspicuous figure in the farmers' revolt, or the populist movement, was Mary Ellen Lease, called

"The Kansas Pythoness." Born in Pennsylvania of Irish parentage, Mrs. Lease, who described herself as a professional radical, gained notoriety by advising the farmers "to raise less corn and more hell." To Ignatius Donnelly, the eloquent "Sage of Ninninger," fell the task of drawing up the first national platform of the Populist Party in 1892. He possessed the Celt's love for language and in the preamble produced a memorable indictment of plutocratic America:

We meet in the midst of a nation brought to the verge of moral, political, and material ruin. Corruption dominates the ballot-box, the Legislatures, the Congress, and touches even the ermine of the bench. The people are demoralized; most of the States have been compelled to isolate the voters at the polling places to prevent universal intimidation or bribery. The newspapers are largely subsidized or muzzled, public opinion silenced, business prostrated, homes covered with mortgages, labor impoverished, and the land concentrating in the hands of capitalists. The urban workmen are denied the right of organization for self-protection, imported pauperized labor beats down their wages, a hireling standing army, unrecognized by our laws, is established to shoot them down, and they are rapidly degenerating into European conditions.

The populists have been accused of an anti-immigrant bias, but one historian of the movement asserts that in Kansas, at least, large numbers of every politically consequential group became active populists, and the party aimed "to attract the political support of organized labor, of tenant farmers, and very likely of Irish-Americans."

Other Irish-Americans, some imbued with a revolutionary tradition as a result of the long history of rebellion against England, played prominent roles in radical organizations. Two of the most prominent leaders in American communism, William Z. Foster and Elizabeth Gurley ("Ma") Flynn, were children of English-hating Irish immigrants. Ma Flynn wrote in her autobiography of her descent from revolutionary forebears in the Emerald Isle:

As children, we drew in a burning hatred of British rule with our mother's milk. Until my father died, at over eighty, he never said *England* without adding, "God damn her!" Before I was ten I knew of the great heroes—Robert Emmet, Wolfe Tone, Michael Davitt, Parnell and O'Donovan Rossa.

Benjamin Gitlow, onetime head of the American Communist Party, admitted that the Irish communist contingent was small but constituted "a virile, aggressive element" boasting of a revolutionary tradition and providing the party with "organizers, writers, editors, speakers, trade union leaders, and valuable contacts with important elements in other trade unions."

Irishmen held key positions in the Industrial Workers of the World, the radical labor organization of the early twentieth century; and what is often regarded as the most violent incident in the history of American labor, the bombing of the *Los Angeles Times* plant on October 1, 1910, was the work of

James B. McNamara, his brother John J. McNamara, and Ortie McManigal. It would be a distortion, of course, to portray the Fosters, Flynns, and Mc-Namaras as representative of the American Irish, but there were enough to discredit any stereotype of a conservative Irish politician.

Moreover, is it really accurate to describe immigrant voters as "usually at odds with the reform aspirations of the American progressives," as Richard Hofstadter does in his provocative study, *The Age of Reform*?—or to assert, as he has, that the big-city machines worked "to limit the range and achievements of progressivism"? Several historians have challenged this conventional portrait of urban politics at the turn of the century. J. Joseph Huthmacher argues that the role of the Yankee-Protestant middle-class reformers has been overstressed to the neglect of other elements. How, he asks, did the progressive movement win important victories in states like New York and Massachusetts "heavily populated with non-Protestant and non-Anglo-Saxon immigrants and sons of immigrants"? The answer is: Progressives won only with the support of men nurtured in the Irish political organizations—individuals like Alfred E. Smith, Robert F. Wagner, Sr., James A. Foley, James Michael Curley, and David I. Walsh. It has now become evident that the bosses, while continuing to engage in the traditional shakedowns and "honest graft," also served from time to time as agencies of change. Under Boss Charles F. Murphy, long-time Tammany chief, the machine cleaned up the police force, curbed prostitution, and helped conflicting ethnic and class groups to live together with less friction than has been true in recent years.

Nearly all Irish-American politicians who have achieved any national prominence were liberals in their own times; nearly all were members of the Democratic Party, an organization with a strong liberal tradition. The career of Alfred E. Smith is illustrative: Born on the Lower East Side of New York, employed in the Fulton Fish Market as a boy, he climbed the Tammany ladder from runner to ward leader to assemblyman to sheriff to governor, and his style is typical of the "Irish politician." When he received the Democratic presidential nomination in 1928, his enemies used his religious and social background against him. In addition to the crude anti-Catholicism that the campaign engendered and the wrath of the prohibitionists over Smith's skeptical attitude toward the Eighteenth Amendment, critics trotted out the well-worn clichés about the "evils of the city." Rural, middle-class America was duly warned of dangers to traditional American virtues. To slanders of the bigots were added the warnings of the genteel reformers. Chief among them was William Allen White, who dubbed Smith the representative of the "saloon, prostitution and gambling"; Smith was the leader of "a group who have back of them only physical appetite and no regard for law or reform."

Not merely unfair, such statements were untrue. Smith, alleged to have "no regard for law or reform," had been the most effective and most progressive governor of his generation, perhaps of the century. As a leader in the state assembly, he joined with Robert F. Wagner, Sr., another Tammany product, to secure a workmen's compensation law, to outlaw child labor, and to write progressive health and housing legislation. As governor, he proved that a loyal machine politician could also be a civil libertarian, vigorously condemning the Republican-controlled legislature of 1920 for denying seats to five legally elected Socialists. He ordered a special election in which the five Socialists again won and were seated. At the height of the big "Red Scare," Smith vetoed various acts of the legislature which had attempted to establish a loyalty test for teachers, create a special agency to search for "criminal anarchy," and restrict academic freedom in private schools. In a veto message Smith declared:

the safety of this government and its institutions rests upon the reasoned loyalty of its people. It does not need for its defense a system of intellectual tyranny which, in the endeavor to choke error by force, must of necessity crush truth as well.

During his eight years as chief executive, New York pioneered a number of social reforms and served as a laboratory for improving the art and science of government. With the help of bright young technocrats, including Robert Moses and Frances Perkins, Smith created a model modern-state bureaucracy. Ironically, in doing so, he undermined an old-style "machine" system, which subsequently lost much of its patronage power.

In retrospect, considering that Smith ran against the nationally known, deeply respected Herbert Hoover at a time when the country was basking in Coolidge prosperity, it is clear that Smith's Roman Catholicism was not the decisive factor in his defeat, although it certainly cost him votes in the South and other sections of the country. He probably ran a better race than any other Democrat could have run. Most significant in the returns is that he did well in the large cities. In 1924, the Republicans had carried the nation's 12 largest cities by 1,300,000 votes; in 1928, attracted by Smith's urban image, the same cities swung to the Democrats by a slight margin. This shift set a pattern for the future; until 1928, the Democrats had not been particularly an urban party. Smith's campaign, however, prepared the way for the city-based and *oriented* party of the New Deal years and after. For this reason, political scientists have taken to describing 1928 as the year of the "Al Smith Revolution."

In the New Deal years, Irish politicians became more visible nationally. As an essential part of the national Democratic coalition, they began to fill important posts in the executive and judicial branches of the government. Franklin Roosevelt appointed his chief political aide, James A. Farley, as Postmaster General, selected Frank Murphy of Michigan to be Attorney-General and later Associate Justice of the Supreme Court, and enlisted Thomas Corcoran, a young, effervescent Celt from Rhode Island, as a speechwriter, special counsel, and general troubleshooter. Roosevelt, the scion of one political dynasty, helped start another when he named Joseph P. Kennedy to the Securities and Exchange Commission and later as Ambassador to London. In the 20 years between 1933 and 1953, eight Irish-Americans served in cabinet posts; in the previous century and a half of the republic, only four had held so high a post. Similarly, Irish-American representation in the national Congress increased substantially. Many Irish, however, remained discontent and disgruntled, continuing to believe that Smith had been rejected because of his religion. They agreed with Farley, a disappointed aspirant for the Democratic presidential nomination in 1940, who complained that a "No Irish Need Apply" notice was posted on the White House.

After the Second World War, more and more Irish began to drift into the Republican Party. Estimates of Irish votes for Dwight Eisenhower in 1956 run as high as 50 percent of the whole. This trend can be explained partly by a rise in economic and social status; like everyone else who could afford it, the Irish deserted the cities for the more conservative suburbs. The loss of voters hit Democratic machines just when effects of welfare programs of the New Deal had begun to erode the very foundations of the machine strength. Edwin O'Connor, in his entertaining and perceptive novel, *The Last Hurrah*, attributed the downfall of the old-time boss (such as James M. Curley of Boston, on whose career he based his story), to one man—Roosevelt: "He destroyed the old-time boss, by taking away his source of power. All over the country the bosses have been dying for the last twenty years, thanks to Roosevelt."

Quite apart from the declining appeal of a five-dollar handout in an era of unemployment compensation and Social Security, the better educated, more affluent middle-class Irish no longer responded to the appeals of the boss to support "your own kind" and were much less tolerant of the "honest graft" that increased their taxes. Further disenchantment with Democrats came as a result of the accusations of a Republican Senator from Wisconsin, Joseph R. McCarthy, that the party was "soft on communism." The Irish, suggests Daniel P. Moynihan, achieved a strong temporary advantage over the Anglo-American establishment during the McCarthy period: "In the era of security clearances, to be an Irish Catholic became *prima facie* evidence of loyalty. Harvard men were to be checked; Fordham men would do the checking."

In 1960, when an Irish Catholic again ran for the presidency, the election was to cause an "identity crisis" for those Irish who were Republicans; for all Irish-Americans it was to become the golden moment of their history.

Sources

Basler, Roy, Editor, *The Collected Works of Abraham Lincoln,* New Brunswick, N. J., 1953.

Benson, Lee, *The Concept of Jacksonian Democracy,* Princeton, N. J., 1961.

Brogan, Denis W., *Politics in America* (paperback edition), New York, 1960.

Connable, Alfred, and Edward Silberfarb, *Tigers of Tammany,* New York, 1967.

Flynn, Elizabeth Gurley, *I Speak My Own Piece,* New York, 1955.

Gibson, Florence E., *The Attitudes of the New York Irish toward State and National Affairs, 1848–1892,* New York, 1951.

Handlin, Oscar, *Al Smith and His America,* Boston, 1958.

Hofstadter, Richard, *The Age of Reform: From Bryan to FDR,* New York, 1955.

Huthmacher, J. Joseph, "Urban Liberalism and the Age of Reform," *Mississippi Valley Historical Review,* Vol. XLIX, September 1962.

Josephson, Matthew and Hannah, *Al Smith: Hero of the Cities,* New York, 1969.

Levine, Edward M., *The Irish and Irish Politicians,* Notre Dame, Ind., 1966.

Lubell, Samuel, *The Future of American Politics,* New York, 1952.

Nugent, Walter T. K., *The Tolerant Populists,* Chicago, 1963.

Ridge, Martin, *Ignatius Donnelly,* Chicago, 1962.

Riordan, William L., *Plunkitt of Tammany Hall* (paperback edition), New York, 1963.

Rosenberg, Marvin and Dorothy, "The Dirtiest Election," *American Heritage,* Vol. XXIII, No. 5, August 1962.

Werner, M. R., *Tammany Hall,* New York, 1928.

White, William Allen, *Masks in a Pageant,* New York, 1928.

Zink, Harold, *City Bosses in the United States: A Study of Twenty Municipal Bosses,* Durham, N. C., 1930.

Chapter Six

Allegiance to Two Flags

In ever-dwindling numbers, veterans of the Easter Rebellion of 1916 march in America's St. Patrick's Day parades. Theirs is an honored place because Irish nationalism is a deeply revered tradition among Irish-Americans. To be sure, interest in European affairs has been characteristic of nearly every immigrant people. In Washington's time, Frenchmen living in Charleston, Philadelphia, and New York enthusiastically supported the French Revolution; in the 1870s, German-Americans gloried in the success of German arms in the Franco-Prussian war; in our own time, we have witnessed the zealous concern of American Jews in the growth of Israel and exiled Cubans in the fate of their island. But no immigrant people has maintained such long and consistent attention to the problems of the old country as the Irish. The *Irish-American Almanac* of 1875 carried a poem by T. D. Sullivan, whose opening lines caught the sentiment of thousands:

> Columbia the free is the land of my birth
> And my paths have all been on American earth
> But my blood is as Irish as any can be,
> And my heart is with Erin afar o'er the sea.

The Irish question was a constant irritant in Anglo-American relations: Hatred of England borne across the Atlantic by the first generation became the legacy of succeeding ones. Other Americans may have regarded Irish agitation over Britain as something quite irrational, but the grievances were real. Britain never extended its significant nineteenth century advances in good government and social reform to Ireland, displaying toward John Bull's other island little of the patience, tolerance, and balance that marked British imperialism at its best. Statesmen normally found on the side of right, progress, and enlightenment had a curious blind spot for the Irish. The latter, in turn, identified England with tyranny, bigotry, and heartlessness; they hated fiercely.

In the United States, where immigrants nurtured their ancient rancor, many talked hopefully of a war of liberation, and felt their opportunity had arrived in the years after the Civil War. Accordingly, they joined the Irish Revolutionary Brotherhood. The announced purpose of the Brotherhood, or "Fenians" as they were called, was the conquest of Canada, a country to be held in hostage until Great Britain had freed Ireland. The Fenians did manage to mount in 1866 and 1870 comic-opera attacks on Canada, with the loud endorsement of those Americans who harbored resentment against Britain for allegedly aiding the Confederacy during the war. Although William Seward, Secretary of State, condemned the Fenian raids as a violation of American neutrality, in Congress there was rather more praise than censure of Fenians, as politicians kept their eye on the Irish vote.

Another, but lesser-known, venture of the Fenians involved the financing of the first two undersea craft built by the father of the modern submarine, the Irish-born John Holland. The inventor had turned to the Fenians after being rebuffed in his efforts to interest the United States Navy in his idea. With money supplied from the Fenian "skirmishing fund," Holland built two boats. The second one, dubbed the *Fenian Ram,* proved quite successful in tests conducted on the Hudson River, near New York City. A dispute between Holland and his revolutionary backers, however, prevented its use for its intended purpose: the destruction of British warships in American harbors.

Interest in Ireland quickened with coincidental emergence of Charles Stewart Parnell as the guiding light of the Irish Land League in Ireland and the appearance of a cluster of dedicated revolutionary leaders in the United States. Chief among them was the man once described as the "Lenin" of Irish-American nationalism, John Devoy. Only 29 years of age when he arrived in New York in January 1871, Devoy was on the threshold of a career spanning 60 years of the Irish freedom movement, making him in the opinion of many Englishmen the most bitter, persistent, and dangerous enemy England ever had. Born in Kill, County Kildare in 1842, the son of a leader in the Young Ireland movement, he joined the Irish Republican Brotherhood in 1861, later served in the French Foreign Legion, was imprisoned by the British for terrorist activities and released on condition that he go into exile in the United States.

Devoy interrupted his career as journalist in America with other activities, such as rescuing a group of Fenian military prisoners from western Australia. From 1881 to 1885, Devoy published the *Irish Nation,* whose failure was partly a result of his support of Blaine's candidacy in 1884. Afterwards, Devoy played a leading role in the extreme revolutionary organization, the *Clan-na-Gael,* and in 1903 founded another journal, the *Gaelic-American,* to propagate its principles.

Other militant leaders included O'Donovan Rossa, an amiable man, but quite adept in the uses of dynamite; John Boyle O'Reilly, the eloquent editor of the *Boston Pilot,* and Patrick Ford, co-owner and editor of New York's *Irish World.* Trained for newspaper work on William Lloyd Garrison's *Liberator,* Ford imitated the famous abolitionist in his immoderate and doctrinaire approach to issues.

These men and others worked to stimulate Irish-American nationalism and were aided by periodic visits of revolutionaries from the Emerald Isle. Michael Davitt always attracted great throngs on his American trips. The most emotional reception of all greeted Parnell on his tour, in 1880, in behalf of the Irish Land League. Within six months, Parnell travelled 16,000 miles in all parts of the country, addressed a joint session of Congress, and raised hundreds of thousands of dollars.

Unfortunately for the nationalist cause, a distinct thaw in Anglo-American relations had commenced after 1870. Before that date, Irish hostility toward Britain conformed with the consensus of American opinion, but the amicable settlement of the Alabama claims dispute marked the beginning of a rapprochement between the two English-speaking countries. The Anglophobia of the Irish now only complicated American policy, and such incidents as the apparent Irish-American sabotage of the Bayard-Chamberlain Treaty of 1888, their belligerency in the Venezuelan boundary dispute of 1893, and the sending by the United Irish Societies of Chicago of an "ambulance corps" of about 60 men to South Africa to aid the rebels during the Boer War incensed those concerned with making American foreign policy. In 1900, when Irish and German complaints against the first Hay-Pauncefote Treaty on the Panama Canal contributed to the treaty's rejection by the Senate, Secretary of State John Hay exploded at "hyphenated Americans," those "idiots" who yelled he was not an American because he did not say "to Hell with the Queen" at every breath.

Nonetheless, although both political parties consistently declared in favor of Irish freedom, and few politicians resisted an occasional thrust at Great Britain, the Irish exerted little real influence on the course of American diplomacy. Other factors operated with the ethnic opposition in the cases of the Bayard-Chamberlain and Hay-Pauncefote treaties, and, in the end, the eternal vigilance and strident declarations of the nationalist spokesmen did little to retard the development of an informal British-American alliance. The relative impotence of the agitation can be partially attributed to the failure of the nationalist leaders to keep the attention of the mass of Irish voters. To be sure, great crowds could be counted on for Irish freedom rallies and outings. Mr. Dooley commented sarcastically, "Be hivins if Ireland cud be freed by a picnic it's not only be free today but an empire." But the ardor stimulated at these festivities usually faded by the dawn.

If never more than a small minority belonged to such moderate organizations as the United Irish League of America, fewer still joined the radical Fenians or the Clan-na-Gael. Constant bickering and factionalism also hurt; little agreement existed among the nationalists on how best to help Ireland. A somewhat united position had been established in the 1880s, but the disgrace and death of Parnell fragmented the Irish party in the United States as much as in Ireland. The Celtic press reflected this division. Devoy's *Gaelic-American* favored revolutionary action; the *Boston Pilot* was usually moderate. The *Irish World* veered toward extremism, but rivalry with the *Gaelic-American* caused it to follow an ambivalent policy as to methods. Such squabbling confused most Irish-Americans and tended to diminish their interest in Ireland.

Until 1914, the nationalists, the men of "the fanatic heart" whose dreams lay overseas, usually had to compete for support with Irish political bosses, whom they could not beat at the game of garnering votes. Unless he found it convenient, the politician usually turned a deaf ear to nationalist appeals. For example, as Thomas N. Brown has pointed out, Cleveland got a high percentage of Irish votes in Brooklyn in 1888, despite the gaffe by Lord Sackville-West. The reason was simple enough. Hugh McLaughlin, the Brooklyn boss, maintained good relations with Cleveland and turned out to vote for him. But just at a time when Irish nationalism appeared to be dormant, the outbreak of World War I reawakened interest, and thrust the question of Irish freedom back into the center of American politics.

When fighting erupted in August 1914, President Woodrow Wilson issued the customary proclamation of American neutrality and appealed to his countrymen to avoid taking sides in the European struggle, asking them to be impartial in thought as well as deed. To advise Americans to "think" impartially was, perhaps, a laudable ideal, but hardly a realistic one. In a nation of immigrants or descendants of immigrants, emotional ties to the old country could not be easily severed. Not even Wilson himself, although he made an earnest effort, remained entirely impartial. By May 1915, he believed that "England is fighting our fight."

Irish-American nationalists reacted to the war in terms of an old revolutionary axiom: "England's difficulty is Ireland's opportunity." The leaders of the Clan-na-Gael, who sent a secret message to Berlin expressing hope "for the success of the German people in the unequal struggle forced upon them," probably did not admire Imperial Germany and its autocratic Protestant Kaiser any more than leaders of the United Irishmen of 1795 endorsed the principles of the French Revolution, but they foresaw the possibility of an independent Ireland emerging out of British defeat. Until the Easter Rebellion of 1916, however, those who openly supported the Central Powers did not speak for the bulk of Irish-Americans. A few Irish, appalled by the "rape of Belgium," saw the greatest immediate danger in the growth of "poison Prussianism." They could not imagine Germany as the champion of the rights of any small nation. Possibly the largest number, while remaining wary of English machinations, thought it unwise to favor either of the belligerent sides. Early in 1916, the British ambassador at Washington, Cecil Spring-Rice, still considered the majority of Irish-Americans favorable to the Allies. He warned London, however, that any untoward incident might easily change this attitude.

The Easter Rebellion of 1916 provided the incident Spring-Rice feared. Not that the American Irish greeted the rising with enthusiasm; most undoubtedly agreed with the United Irish League's denunciation of the poorly planned rebellion as "needless letting of good Irish blood." But the ruthless ferocity with which the British repressed the revolt shocked them as it did nearly everyone in the United States. Membership increased substantially in the recently formed Friends of Irish Freedom, whose announced object was "to encourage and assist any movement that will tend to bring about the national independence of Ireland." This organization quickly developed into the largest and most effective of all the Irish-American pressure groups.

Failure of the Wilson administration to register a strong protest against the Dublin executions was hotly resented by the Irish; some nationalist leaders expressed their hurt and annoyance by working against Wilson's reelection in 1916. The President did not help matters when he injected the issue of hyphenism into the campaign by referring critically to the patriotism of some of the foreign-born and speaking sharply about people who needed "hyphens in their name" because their hearts had not crossed the Atlantic with them. It was an impolitic remark, implying that ties of sentiment to an individual's country of origin undermined his loyalty to the United States.

Furthermore, those who had taken up the cry of hyphenism usually confined their indictment solely to the Irish- or German-Americans. The term was never applied to the large number of Anglo-Americans sympathetic to the Allies. The American minister in London, Walter Hines Page, without any apparent embarrassment, simultaneously could condemn one type of hyphenism and encourage another: "We Americans," he urged, "have to throw away our provincial ignorance . . . , hang our Irish agitators and shoot our hyphenates and bring up our children with reverence for English history and in awe of English literature."

Particularly disaffected with Wilson were Devoy, who characterized him as "the meanest and most malignant man" who ever filled the office of President of the United States, and Judge Daniel P. Cohalan, a founder of the Friends of Irish Freedom. Bad feeling between the President and Cohalan dated from the Democratic National Convention of 1912 when Cohalan had strenuously opposed Wilson's nomination. Whether Devoy, Cohalan, and other nationalist leaders succeeded in siphoning off any significant Irish votes from Wilson in the 1916 election is debatable. It is true, as several students of the election have shown, that Wilson failed to carry a single state where there was a sizable Irish population. On the other hand, he did very well in the Irish areas of New York City and by an overwhelming vote carried Boston, a traditional seat of Irish power. Wilson personally believed that Irish politicians had "double-crossed" him, and this belief served to heighten his antagonism to Irish demands.

Five months after his reelection, Wilson went before a joint session of Congress to ask for a declaration of war against Germany. Up to the hour that the President delivered his war message many German-Americans and, to a lesser extent, Irish-Americans tried to preserve the nation's neutrality by urging congressmen to vote against a declaration of war and by participating in demonstrations for peace in major cities. After Congress had made the decision for war, John Devoy spoke for a good number of Irish-Americans in charging that an unpopular war had been thrust upon a browbeaten Congress by an autocratic president.

Considering the controversies of the neutrality years, such a reaction is hardly surprising. But it did not last long. The Irish and all the other immigrant peoples without exception soon put themselves wholeheartedly into the war effort. The Irish regiment of New York, the "Fighting Sixty Ninth," under the command of "Wild Bill" Donovan, was one of the first American units to reach France and before long newspaper stories had begun the process of making immortal the regiment's chaplain, the revered Father Duffy.

Of course, some Irish adjusted only with difficulty to the new relationship between the United States and its ally Great Britain. For a few diehards, accommodation with "perfidious Albion" proved impossible. Jeremiah O'Leary, founder of the anti-British American Truth Society, found himself jailed under the Espionage Act for continuing his attacks upon John Bull. The Friends of Irish Freedom came under suspicion when both Theodore Roosevelt and John Purroy Mitchel, mayor of New York City and grandson of the Irish hero of the rebellion of 1848, accused Devoy and Judge Cohalan of disloyalty. Officials in the Wilson administration were convinced that Cohalan had indulged in treasonable activity. In September 1917, Secretary of State Robert Lansing released to the *New York World* certain documents that seemed to indicate that the judge had been in the pay of Berlin. The Justice Department tried unsuccessfully to obtain conclusive evidence against Cohalan, and there were rumors of an investigation by the New York State Legislature, but no action was ever taken.

Devoy strongly defended Cohalan in the *Gaelic-American* and refused to stop his attacks on the "Anglomaniacs." At times, Postmaster-General Albert S. Burleson felt Devoy's paper and other Irish publications, such as the *Irish World* and the *Freeman's Journal,* went too far in their criticism of England. During the course of the war he banned them from the mail on several occasions for publishing "seditious" remarks.

Burleson's conception of sedition was remarkable. He censored the *Irish World* for expressing its belief that England would renege on its promise to create a Jewish state in Palestine, and for describing French life and ideals as materialistic. The *Freeman's Journal* offended by reprinting Jefferson's remark that Ireland should be a republic. In September 1918, the *Gaelic-American* lost its second-class mailing privileges, apparently because Burleson objected to Devoy's handling of an interview granted by Wilson to the widow of an Irish pacifist and to the paper's approval of a resolution on Irish freedom introduced in Congress by Jeanette Rankin of Montana. Generally, however, incidents of war censorship of this brand were exceptional.

With the signing of the Armistice, Irish nationalists turned with anticipation to the Peace Conference at Paris, because it appeared that an independent Ireland might well emerge from the deliberations. Because the peacemakers of 1919 were primarily concerned with drawing up a peace between Germany and the Allies, the Irish question might therefore seem irrelevant. Yet, the Irish asked themselves: Had not President Wilson in his Fourteen Points and subsequent proposals for a just and enduring peace emphasized that "national aspirations" must be respected and all peoples given the "right of self-determination"? Naturally enough, they interpreted such remarks to mean an *independent* Ireland. Cohalan went so far as to declare the President and the Congress of the United States "are determined to see that Ireland shall be included with other countries among those to whom the right of self-determination shall be given." Such a conclusion was understandable; the Irish could not believe that Wilson's declaration on self-determination applied only to Poland, Czechoslovakia, Yugoslavia, and "other places with unpronounceable names."

Wilson no doubt regretted the construction placed by the Irish, upon his remarks, but his unguarded rhetoric certainly had contributed to their optimism, and to the intensity of the resentment that followed upon the failure of the peace negotiations to consider the Irish question. Moreover, the President dealt rather brusquely with the American Commission for Irish Independence, a trio of prominent Irish-Americans who had hastened to Paris in a futile attempt to secure a formal hearing for the Irish cause before the peace conference. Doubting their good faith, the President charged the Commissioners with "mischief-making" and in the process alienated nearly all of Irish America.

When Wilson returned from Paris to seek approval of the Versailles Treaty, he encountered strong opposition from the vast majority of politically active Irish leaders. With Italian- and German-Americans, also disgruntled with terms of the settlement, the Irish joined ranks in a crusading campaign to defeat the Wilsonian peace. Their efforts convinced many Americans of the justice of their grievances, and others, dismayed at the bewildering babble of charges and countercharges, concluded that the United States entry into the League of Nations would turn every dispute in that organization touching upon the homeland of an immigrant group into a domestic political quarrel. Most significantly, politicians dependent upon ethnic votes found support of the Versailles Treaty a risky business. At the very least, protests of the Irish and other hyphenate groups helped create a sentiment in the country for certain reservations about the treaty which Wilson would not accept.

After the final rejection of the treaty by the Senate in March 1920, the nationalist leaders turned their attention to the presidential election of that year and helped persuade hundreds of thousands of Irish Democrats to desert their party. The Irish delivered a sweeping protest vote against James M. Cox, the Democratic candidate, whom they had identified with Wilson's peace program. John Devoy rejoiced at the blow that had been dealt to pro-English schemings; with their ballots the Irish-Americans had punished "all the Anglomaniacs, international financiers and British agents."

Clearly, the defeat of the treaty and the election of Warren Harding did not directly advance the cause of Irish freedom, but for two years the Irish question had been thrust into the center of American politics, had gained wide attention and a largely sympathetic reaction. Even confirmed Anglophiles came to realize that truly harmonious relations between the United States and Great

Britain depended upon a settlement in Ireland. Nineteen state governors, Samuel Gompers, president of the American Federation of Labor, and publisher William Randolph Hearst joined many other prominent Americans in accepting membership on the American Committee for Relief in Ireland. The Committee protested against British militarism in Ireland and in 1921 raised over five million dollars in relief funds. Irish-American nationalism reached its zenith in numbers, respectability, and financial power.

Then, quite suddenly, the long struggle ended. British Prime Minister David Lloyd-George decided it might be more politic to conciliate the Irish rather than coerce them. In June 1921, he opened negotiations with Irish nationalist leaders in London. In December, a treaty was signed granting virtual independence to Ireland save for the six counties of Ulster which remained in union with Great Britain. Vestiges of Irish-American nationalism and Anglophobia continued throughout the next two decades and, indeed, have not completely disappeared even today, as the excitement over the Ulster riots of 1970 has demonstrated. But the Anglo-Irish treaty of 1921 did effectively remove the Irish question from American politics.

The work of the nationalist was finished, but the activity he inspired, from holiday picnics to letter writing, mass rallies, fund raising, and electoral pressures not only prepared the way for freedom of the mother country but helped to mold the Irish into a force to be reckoned with in American life.

Sources

Brown, Thomas N., *Irish-American Nationalism, 1870–1890*, Philadelphia, 1966.

D'Arcy, William, *The Fenian Movement in the United States, 1858–1886*, Washington, D.C., 1947.

Duff, John B., "The Versailles Treaty and the Irish-Americans," *Journal of American History*, Vol. LV, No. 3, December 1968.

Hendrick, Burton J., *The Life and Letters of Walter H. Page*, Garden City, N.Y., 1925.

Tansill, Charles C., *America and the Fight for Irish Freedom, 1866–1922*, New York, 1957.

Ward, Alden J., *Ireland and Anglo-American Relations, 1899–1921*, Toronto, 1969.

Chapter Six

Chapter Seven

The Irish, God,
and the Devil

Historically, the Irish have been a people deeply concerned with religion. When St. Patrick brought Christianity to the pagan Celts, they embraced it with astonishing speed and before long were sending enthusiastic missionaries off to carry the new faith to the hinterlands of Europe. The establishment of the Church of England during the Reformation only served to intensify Irish devotion to Rome and added a strong ingredient to Irish nationalism. Religion became one more aspect of a culture to be defended against oppressors. Despite the prominence of Protestants in the nationalist movement—Wolfe Tone, Robert Emmet, and Charles Parnell, to mention only the most famous—the people identified Catholicism so closely with Irish nationhood as to make the two terms virtually synonymous.

Moreover, as was the case with nearly all the immigrant peoples, migration to America strengthened these religious convictions. Newcomers had to make adjustments to life in the United States. They had to shed one old habit after another, learn new occupations after adopting a radically different life style—but they refused to be separated from their old-country faith.

In the United States, the Catholic Church that the famine Irish found was hardly more than a mission skiff on a vast sea of Protestantism. In a hundred years it would become the largest single religious denomination in the country, and the wealthiest, most stable branch of world Catholicism. The Irish did not accomplish this alone; later immigrants—Italians, Poles, Czechs, Hungarians —provided a good part of the numerical growth, as did an accelerating birth rate. But the Irish provided the leadership. From the beginning of their emigration, the Irish brought with them their priests, who before long greatly outnumbered the English and French emigré clergymen who had been ministering to the country's few Catholics. Inevitably, from the large numbers of Irish priests, bishops were selected; within a generation of the great migration, the Irish dominated the American hierarchy. Thirty-five of the 69 bishops of the United States in 1886 were Irish. Although by then the newer immigrants had begun demanding bishops of their own nationalities, the Irish dominance of the leadership persisted; of 18 bishops in the New York metropolitan area in 1961, one was Chinese and one was Italian: the rest were Irish.

The enormous growth of the Catholic Church through immigrant stimulus caused concern among older Americans. Even the old, aristocratic Catholic leaders of Maryland were unhappy about hordes of Irish communicants the Church had gained. They much preferred to have the Church grow slowly, taking time to assimilate its gains. But their disquiet was as nothing compared to the alarm of some Protestant leaders. Anti-Catholic feelings were endemic in America, having arrived with the earliest settlers. In colonial times, preachers railed against the Roman Church, "the whore of Babylon," or the Pope, the "tyrant of the triple tiara." In New England (where Pope's Day became an annual holiday devoted to noisy parades and the burning of the Pope's effigy), "No Popery" became a slogan of the American Revolution. Nevertheless, in most colonies, Catholics could live in peace, prejudice usually being limited to oratorical exercises. Various colonies did enact laws restricting Catholics, but careful research has shown that such laws were seldom enforced rigorously.

In the nineteenth century, as the Catholic population steadily rose, denunciations of the Popish menace grew apace. Lyman Beecher, one of the most formidable preachers of the 1820s, warned about a conspiracy to make the old Northwest a fief of Rome! Samuel F. B. Morse, the well-known artist and future inventor of the telegraph, whose native New England animus against Catholicism had been aggravated by an incident in Rome when a Swiss Guard had indignantly knocked Morse's hat from his head during a papal procession, presented a most complete indictment of alleged papal subversion in two volumes, entitled *Foreign Conspiracy against the Liberties of the United States* and *Imminent Danger to the Free Institutions of the United States.* If educated men like Beecher and Morse could indulge so readily in such flights of fantasy, it is hardly surprising that others were led into acts of violence to combat the Catholic menace. In 1834, a mob burned down a convent school in Charleston, Massachusetts. So strong was the prejudice in the area that no attempt was made to arrest the ringleaders of the mob.

Fears of Catholic power were not, however, entirely irrational. Many Protestants who did not believe in the apocryphal stories of the Pope's plans for America and deplored arson as a means of persuasion nonetheless remained suspicious of the Catholic Church. One disturbing issue concerned lay control of parishes. In nearly all Protestant denominations, the congregation chose the minister, determining his salary and dismissing him if he proved unsatisfactory to its members. Catholic canon law, on the other hand, vested the right of appointing and relieving pastors solely in the bishops. Lay trustees had been appointed or elected in many parishes, however, to assist in the temporal work of administration, and trouble often developed when Catholics of one nationality attempted to remove a pastor of a different ethnic background and to replace him with one of their own. To Protestants, this seemed a reasonable procedure, so when the trustees of St. Louis Church in Buffalo, New York, rebelled against their bishop, nativist opinion sided with them, as did the New York State Legislature, which enacted the Putnam Bill in 1855, requiring lay ownership of all church property and prohibiting a clergyman from holding property in his own name.

The Putnam Act was a victory for the nativists as well as for the lay trustees, but it was not destined to be a permanent one. John Hughes, the new Archbishop of New York, a native of Ireland who had come to the United States in 1817, began a long but ultimately successful struggle, with the support of his immigrant flock, to permit the vesting of Church property in a bishop or his appointees. He won his battle in 1863 when the manpower needs of the Union Army persuaded the New York legislature to repeal the Putnam Act because it had antagonized so many potential Catholic recruits.

As controversial as was Hughes's position on trusteeism, it was a molehill compared to the mountainous furor he raised among nativists and others, with his battle against the Public School Society, a semiprivate organization controlling New York City's educational system. Under the Society's administration, Protestant prayers and hymns began the school day and the King James Bible was prominently displayed and recited; some texts contained such pejoratives as "the Pope, that man of Sin." At first Hughes sought a share of public school funds for parochial schools, thus initiating an issue continuing to generate controversy even today. But after going so far as to run a Catholic ticket in the 1841 city elections, he realized the hopelessness of obtaining public funds, and then worked closely with Governor William H. Seward to secure the disestablishment of the Public School Society. The Spencer Bill of 1842 accomplished this goal by putting the New York City school system under the supervision of elected school commissioners, a policy adopted elsewhere throughout the United States.

John Hughes was the first prominent member of the hierarchy that the immigrant Irish produced. He won their respect and admiration in the school controversy, and his standing among them became unshakable when, following the destruction of two churches and hundreds of Catholic homes in Philadelphia, he warned the mayor of New York to keep the city's nativists under control. Otherwise, he would not hesitate to use force against them, declaring, "If a single Catholic Church were burned in New York, the city would become a second Moscow." Thoughtful Americans were by then experiencing sober second thoughts about nativism. Appalled by the Philadelphia riots, Philip Hone, an aristocratic New Yorker whose diary is a prime source for the history of the city in the mid-nineteenth century, and who a few years earlier had applauded the election of a nativist mayor of New York, now wrote, "I shan't be caught voting a 'native' ticket again in a hurry."

The temperament and social condition of the Irish probably required Hughes's consistently belligerent attitude toward Protestants, but at times he seemed to deliberately provoke anti-Catholic and anti-Irish feelings. In November 1850, after nativism had somewhat receded before the larger issues of Oregon, the Mexican War, and the reopened slavery controversy, he caused unnecessary pique with an address entitled "The Decline of Protestantism and Its Causes," in which he proclaimed the Catholic mission to convert the world. Such insensitivity contributed to the growth of the Know-Nothing political venture described earlier.

An able but narrow man, Hughes was in many ways the prototype of the conservative Irish prelate: distrustful of non-Catholics, wary of liberalism (to say nothing of revolution), and extremely straight-laced on questions of morality. The puritanism of the Irish gave a cast to American Catholicism that has been a source of concern and dismay to generations of religious liberals. It undoubtedly has caused numerous defections from the Church. Countless thousands, raised as James T. Farrell was, in the traditional Catholic environment, rebelled as did the author of *Studs Lonigan* against the sectarianism, the Jansenism, the sentimentalism of the Irish-Catholic community. A Protestant critic, Peter Viereck, asked, "Is the honorable adjective 'Roman Catholic' truly merited by America's middle class Jansenist Catholicism, puritanized and Calvinized and dehydrated?"

Various explanations have been advanced to account for the fiercely puritanical nature of Irish Catholicism. Part of it unquestionably derives from the influence of Maynooth Seminary, established in Ireland in 1795 by the English Prime Minister, William Pitt the Younger, who wished to discourage the recruitment of priests from Revolutionary France. The Maynooth faculty soon came to be dominated by priests of Jansenist persuasion.

Jansenism, a Catholic heresy originating in France in the seventeenth century, accepted the Calvinist doctrine of predestination in an excessive form, added many other trappings of puritanism, and tended to instill in its adherents an extreme scrupulosity. Although condemned by Rome, the ideas of the sect survived within the Church, and through the influence of Maynooth permeated the Irish Church.

But there were other reasons. The defensive posture of the Irish Church, continually under assault by English Protestants, created a siege mentality. Because it was essential that there should be no compromise with the English heretics, revolutionary nationalism had the paradoxical effect of strengthening religious conservatism.

Certain peculiarly American factors must also be considered. For one thing, all the country's religions that drew heavily upon an immigrant constituency exhibited puritanical and conservative tendencies to some degree. After studying the experience of German and Scandinavian Lutheran groups in the Middle West, Marcus Hansen concluded that the ceremony of these congregations developed a "spontaneous immigrant puritanism" in order to win the approval of older Americans:

The process of Puritanization can be followed by anyone who studies the records of a congregation or the minutes of a synod. Discipline became more and more strict. One after the other, social pleasures that were brought from the Old World fell under the ban. Temperance and Sunday observance were early enforced; then card playing and dancing were prohibited. Simplicity in dress and manners of living became prime virtues.

Some observers have perceived a geographical component in Irish religious conservatism. The hierarchy of New York, for example, traditionally adopted a conservative position. While conceding that such views may have been caused primarily by accidents of personality, William V. Shannon argues that it was in New York that the Irish first captured political power and held it for a long time:

There they first built up a substantial group of upper middle class property owners. The fact that Irish Catholics were almost a majority and had property subtly conditioned the outlook of the Irish clergy running the Catholic Church in New York.

There is surely some truth in this view. At the end of the nineteenth century, when liberal Catholicism began to emerge, the New York hierarchy clung most tenaciously to conservative positions; their progressive protagonists usually had begun careers in the hinterlands. James Cardinal Gibbons of Baltimore, for example, began his episcopal career in the mission territory of North Carolina, then served as Bishop of Richmond, Virginia, an area of few Catholics, before moving to Baltimore in 1877. His great ally in the struggle against the New York conservatives was Archbishop John Ireland, of the frontier diocese of St. Paul. An Irish-born prelate who had emigrated to Minnesota at the age of fifteen and prepared for his ecclesiastical career in France, Ireland was in the forefront of efforts to persuade Catholics to leave Eastern cities for the open land of the West.

At the time of the Third Plenary Council of the American Church at Baltimore in 1884, Gibbons and Ireland stood out as proponents of the liberal movement within the Church. Exactly what liberalism meant is not easy to define; generally, liberals stressed the compatibility of Catholicism with the ideals of American democracy, including the principle of separation of church and state. They also exhibited a friendlier attitude to their fellow Americans of different faiths than did the conservatives. This definition does not suggest, however, as conservatives unfairly charged, that men like Gibbons and Ireland advocated accommodation in matters of Catholic dogma and morals in order to make the Church more palatable to prospective converts. But they did abhor the "ghetto" thinking of Catholics living in the United States; they wanted their coreligionists to break out of cultural isolation of the Catholic community and join with non-Catholics in secular organizations. Bishop John Lancaster Spalding of Peoria summed up the progressive position when he urged Catholics to stop behaving like men in a besieged fortress who talked largely to each other in accents that the world around them seldom heard.

To the conservatives who found their strongest voices in Archbishop Michael Corrigan of New York City and Bernard McQuaid, Bishop of Rochester, this kind of talk approached heresy and for a generation they fought against it. A battle was waged on several fronts and both sides showed typical Irish pugnacity. At times, McQuaid was quite petty. He particularly resented Gibbons' wide popularity and the numerous references in the press to the Cardinal of Baltimore as the leader of American Catholics. "This everlasting talk about the head of the American Church angers me," he wrote to Corrigan. "The good little man can't see that he is making himself ridiculous." McQuaid's jealousy is understandable; less so was his accusation that Archbishop Ireland had been paid half a million dollars to support the Republican Party! True enough, he was a G.O.P. stalwart. Learning that Gibbons had been invited to give the invocation at a Democratic National Convention, he cautioned his friend, "Be on your guard while invoking blessing upon the Democratic convention. Pray hard for the country, not so much for the party." Ireland could be politic, yet to charge him with being on the Republican payroll was both false and malicious.

The dispute within the Irish hierarchy revolved around issues political and social as well as ecclesiastical. One of the chief points of friction concerned the Knights of Labor. Founded in 1869 by Uriah Stephens, the labor organization had gained the bulk of its early membership from Irish Catholics. What alarmed the conservatives were the secret oaths and fixed rituals which Stephens, acting from a mixture of practical, religious, and psychological reasons, had drawn up for the order. The Catholic Church had historically opposed Freemasonry and other secret societies, yet the oaths included enough religious phrasing to lend some credence to the conservatives' fears of heretical activity or worse. Moreover, memories of the recently discredited Molly Maguires made any secret meetings of workingmen suspect. Allan Pinkerton, the founder of the famous strikebreaking detective agency, whose own judgment must be somewhat suspect, since his business depended upon stirring up fear of labor uprisings, contributed to the public misunderstanding by describing the Knights of Labor as "an amalgamation of the Molly Maguires and the Commune." At least one priest in the Pennsylvania anthracite region warned his congregation against joining the Knights.

Realizing the serious threat to the organization's growth that opposition from the Church would mean, the leadership of the Knights took steps to reduce the secrecy and eliminate some of the religious aura surrounding its ritual. When Terence V. Powderly, an Irish Catholic, succeeded Stephens as Master Grand Workman in 1879, he immediately began a correspondence with members of the clergy all over the country, seeking to assure them that membership in the Knights of Labor was in no way incompatible with full communion with the Church. Powderly acted none too soon, for in Canada, the Archbishop of Quebec had secured a condemnation of the Knights from the Vatican.

At the 1884 Plenary Council, the conservatives, led by Archbishop Corrigan, sought to get the Canadian decree extended to the United States. Corrigan, in fact, expressed the opinion that the Knights of Labor were already "undoubtedly forbidden" in both countries; Catholics who refused to quit the order should be denied the sacraments. The proposed condemnation alarmed Gibbons, for he saw the danger of a repetition in the United States of the Church's scandal in Europe: the loss of the working class to the faith. In addition, instinctively, he abhorred the use of authoritarian clerical pronouncements in dealing with social problems. "The whole mentality of James Gibbons reacted against harsh and unnecessary condemnations at any time," wrote his biographer, Msgr. John Tracy Ellis.

It was Gibbons' way to win all men if at all possible through persuasion and kindness, not to alienate them through hasty and unsympathetic use of ecclesiastical authority. This reasonable approach was in entire conscience with man's nature. Gibbons was comfortable in the atmosphere of conciliation, but he felt estranged when the discussion of differences lost that spirit and assumed the air of uncompromising dogmatism.

Powderly was invited by Gibbons to Baltimore, where he gave assurances that he personally was not a Mason but a practicing Catholic, and that none of the principles of the order were at variance with Catholic teaching. Gibbons then embarked for Rome to secure what many called the impossible, a reversal of a decision by the Holy Office of the Vatican. With the aid of Cardinal Manning of England, he succeeded. In spirited interviews, he warned the members of the Papal Curia that working-class defections from Catholicism could be expected if the Church insisted upon depriving workers of their "only means of defense" against the great monopolies: "To lose the heart of the people would be a misfortune for which the friendship of the few rich and powerful would be no compensation." The decision to rehabilitate the Knights appalled clerical conservatives, although in a few years they were able to gloat over the decline and eventual demise of the order.

Yet, the struggle continued on other fronts, and, on the whole, the liberals were successful. By their intercession, Gibbons and Ireland helped to bring about the reinstatement of Father Edward McGlynn, who first had been silenced and then excommunicated by Archbishop Corrigan in 1887 for vigorously endorsing the "socialistic land theories" of Henry George. Corrigan had even tried to get George's famous work *Progress and Poverty* placed on the Index of Prohibited Books. Again the liberals resisted, and under their pressure the Vatican reconsidered the McGlynn case; Ireland was assigned to interview the controversial cleric. Now it was Ireland's turn to gloat at the chance to lay Corrigan low. Gleefully he wrote, "I think the McGlynn case will be reopened with a splendid chance for the poor man. This will break Corrigan's heart." Gibbons, Ireland, and Bishop John Keane of Richmond also won Rome's approval—over strenuous conservative objections—to establish the Catholic University of America. The liberal Keane was installed as its first rector.

Although conservatives felt themselves vindicated in 1899, when Pope Leo XIII issued the letter *Testem Benevolentia,* summarizing the dangers of certain errors that had come to be known as "Americanism," including the idea that the Church must adapt itself to modern civilization, Gibbons would not accept the letter as a rebuke. "This doctrine, which I deliberately call extravagant and absurd, this Americanism as it is called," he replied to the Pope, "has nothing in common with the views, aspirations, doctrine and conduct of Americans." Today no student of the Church subscribes to the thesis that its liberals espoused heretical doctrines; most agree with Robert D. Cross that Gibbons, Ireland, Keane, and others

were among the first to see the real meaning of the experience of the American Church, and to realize the great possibilities that lay open to Catholics if they would approach culture with confidence and charity, or, as Archbishop Ireland might have put it, liberally.

Even while the liberal-conservative imbroglio divided the bishops, Irish monopoly of the hierarchy came under challenge from Central, Southern, and Eastern European Catholics who had been coming to the United States in ever increasing numbers after 1880. The Germans, Bohemians, Croats, Italians, Hungarians, Slovaks, Poles, Slovenes, and Lithuanians crowding into the cities of America were anxious to reestablish the Catholic Church exactly as they knew it in the Old World: an anchor of stability in an ocean of swirling change. But the Church they found in America was puzzling: It seemed more Irish than Catholic.

New immigrants wanted their own parishes, priests who spoke their language, and bishops with an awareness and appreciation of their culture. They demanded "national churches" to serve each of the many different ethnic groups. Nothing else could bring them the Old World satisfactions of religion. In this respect, Catholic immigrants differed not at all from Protestants and Jews who also strove to reconstruct familiar ways of worship in the New World. That immigration is most responsible for the great variety of religious denominations can readily be gathered from such names as the Polish National Church, the Free Magyar Reform Church, or the Armenian Church of North America.

German-Americans, long resentful of Irish clericalism, spearheaded the movement to obtain official sanction for the national churches. In 1890, Peter Cahensly, a German intensely concerned over the condition of his coreligionists in America, warned Rome of the dangers of losing large numbers of immigrants to the faith unless each immigrant group was allowed to have separate parishes with priests of its own nationality. Cahensly did not ask, as has sometimes been alleged, for a reorganization of the hierarchy on a basis of nationality rather than geography; what he did seek was that each group should be represented in the hierarchy by its own bishops.

Cahensly's proposal appealed to newer immigrants, who had additional reasons for resenting the Irish. In city after city, they found the Irish in control of everything: jobs, politics, even the Church. Tactless Irish priests and bishops often worsened relations with their new laity by scarcely concealing their contempt for the newcomers, complaining about the failure of the Italians to make financial contributions to the Church, the anticlericalism of the Czechs, or the clannishness of the French-Canadians. In 1904, when the Chicago Board of Education, under pressure from the Irish clergy, rejected a suggestion from the Italian community that a school be named after the anticlerical Italian patriot Garibaldi, an Italian-language newspaper, noting that three Chicago schools had been named after Irish saloonkeepers, commented bitterly: "If the Italians wished to name the school in Polk Street after some fishvendor from Naples or Sicilian ragpicker, oh, that would be different, but the name of Garibaldi is a truly risky thing." Two years later, *Le Messager,* a French-Canadian journal in Maine, probably raised some Celtic eyebrows when it charged that Irish priests were trying "to Saxonize the French Canadians."

On the question of the national churches, the Irish hierarchy, whether of liberal or conservative persuasion, stood united. Their opposition can be partly explained by a reluctance to give up any of the ecclesiastical power they enjoyed, but they also saw the Cahensly proposal as a threat to the fundamental unity and catholicity of the Irish. Most significantly, however, they feared an adverse reaction from Protestant Americans. To many, national churches would have implied an unwillingness of Catholic immigrants to become assimilated. After Gibbons had denounced Cahensly's attempt to interfere in the lives of German-American Catholics, President Benjamin Harrison complimented him for his stand against "foreignism." Gibbons had helped demonstrate the loyalty of Catholics to the republic, and Irish-Americans fastened on this argument in persuading the Vatican to reject the national church concept.

Still, there were things even Rome could not ordain. What had been denied in theory had to be permitted in practice. When the Italians of the North End of Boston, against the wishes of their Irish superior, insisted on having their own priests and parish, they eventually got their way. Just as Irish politicians learned to accommodate themselves to the demands of their new immigrant constituencies, so the more prudent of the bishops permitted Italian or Ukranian or Polish churches. To refuse was to run the risk of wholesale defections as had occurred in Scranton, Buffalo, and Chicago, cities where, after conflicts with Irish bishops, some Polish parishes united to form the Polish National Church, the only significant and enduring schism in American Catholicism.

By the 1920s (when one estimate places the number of Irish at about 25 percent of the Catholics in America) one can no longer talk logically of an "Irish-American" church. True, for another 40 years the Irish continued to supply more priestly vocations than any other nationality, thus insuring themselves a disproportionate voice in the management of the church, but it becomes difficult to describe specific attributes of the modern church as distinctively Irish.

Yet certain characteristics, such as the puritanism previously discussed, are identifiably so. The organizational abilities which enabled the Irish-American to excel in politics counted just as heavily in administering dioceses and parishes; the church's vaunted reputation for efficiency is largely an Irish inheritance. So, also, is the democratic tone of Catholicism in this country. The famous Catholic English historian, Christopher Dawson, viewed the democratic character of American Catholicism as the first thing that struck a foreign observer. He thought this not entirely a product of American conditions but largely due to Irish influences.

Observers have also noted the relative absence of anticlericalism in the United States. The tradtiion of solidarity between priest and people that obtained in Ireland crossed the Atlantic. "In the United States as in Ireland," writes the eminent historian of the American Church, Msgr. John Tracy Ellis, "the priest was the impoverished immigrant's best friend . . . there was forged between them a union that endured to our own time." In recent years, with the laity much better educated than they were even a generation ago, and when there is, in the wake of the Second Vatican Council, a greater emphasis on lay participation in the church, strains in the relationship have appeared, but these difficulties are slight compared to the virulent anticlericalism of France or Italy.

The Irish, in short, have made incomparable contributions to American Catholicism. The church, in turn, helped them with a proud and splendid spiritual inheritance that bestowed upon the immigrant a sense of security and confidence. No matter how sharp the barbs of Protestant America, no matter how low their social or economic status, the Irish had a secret satisfaction in believing themselves numbered among the chosen people. Unfortunately, this satisfaction too readily expressed itself in a rigid and parochial sectarianism, a distrust of everything "non-Catholic."

Perhaps the election of John F. Kennedy to the presidency possessed a significance more profound than merely the ending of the traditional taboos against a Catholic in the White House. Kennedy did much to blunt old antagonisms between Catholics and other Americans and helped his coreligionists and non-Catholics to grow in understanding and respect of each other. Lawrence Fuchs has written that, by his life, as the hero of a culture, Kennedy had helped

to broaden the basis of consensus in American life by encouraging the forces of encounter within American Catholicism, and by opening the minds of non-Catholics to new opportunities for human communication, learning and growth in dialogue with Catholics.

Sources

Barry, Colman J., *The Catholic Church and German Americans,* Washington, 1953.
Billington, Ray A., *The Protestant Crusade, 1800–1860,* New York, 1938.

Browne, Henry J., *The Catholic Church and the Knights of Labor,* Washington, 1949.

Cross, Robert D., *The Emergence of Liberal Catholicism in America,* Cambridge, Mass., 1958.

Dawson, Christopher, *The Crisis in Western Education,* New York, 1961.

Ellis, John T., *The Life of James Cardinal Gibbons, Archbishop of Baltimore, 1834–1921,* Milwaukee, 1952.

———, "St. Patrick in America" *American Benedictine Review,* Vol. 12, December 1961, pp. 415–429.

———, *American Catholicism,* Revised Edition, Chicago, 1969.

Fuchs, Lawrence H., *John F. Kennedy and American Catholicism,* New York, 1967.

Hansen, Marcus Lee, *The Immigrant in American History* (paperback edition), New York, 1964.

Maynard, Theodore, *The Story of American Catholicism,* 2 vols., New York, 1960.

Nevins, Allan, Editor, *The Diary of Philip Hane,* New York, 1927.

Van Deusen, Glyndon G., "Seward and the School Question Reconsidered," *Journal of American History,* Vol. LII, No. 1, September 1965.

Epilogue

On January 20, 1961, John Fitzgerald Kennedy took the oath of office as thirty-fifth President of the United States. It was the supreme moment in the history of Irish America. As William V. Shannon has said, to a people as committed to politics as the American Irish, Kennedy's victory was "a deeply satisfying accomplishment in which every Irishman could take vicarious pleasure." The election eradicated the resentment of Al Smith's defeat in 1928 and "removed any lingering sense of social inferiority and insecurity." Even conservative Irish Republicans who had worked for Kennedy's opponent, Richard Nixon, were at least able to derive some satisfaction from the breaking of the anti-Catholic tradition.

John Kennedy realized that his religion might be an electoral liability, but unlike Smith, who had believed that bigotry had defeated him, he was never defensive about it. He made light of the 1928 campaign when speaking at the Alfred E. Smith Memorial Dinner in New York in 1959:

I think it well that we recall at this annual dinner what happened to a great governor when he became a presidential nominee. Despite his successful record as a governor, despite his plainspoken voice, the campaign was a debacle. His views were distorted, he carried fewer states than any candidate in his party's history. He lost states which had been solid for his party for half a century or more. To top it off, he lost his own state which he had served so well as governor. You all know his name and religion—Alfred M. Landon, Protestant.

Kennedy was an entirely different type of Irishman than Smith. Cool, urbane, and sophisticated, he spoke with a Harvard accent rather than an East

Side twang. Yet he was thoroughly Celtic. Irishness remained a vital element in his constitution, according to Arthur M. Schlesinger, Jr., his presidential aide and biographer. "It came out in so many ways—in the quizzical wit, the eruptions of boisterous humor, the relish for politics, the love of language; the romantic sense of history, the admiration for physical daring, the toughness, the joy in living, the view of life as comedy and as tragedy."

Ideologically, Kennedy called himself "a pragmatic liberal"; "a Northern Democrat with some sense of restraint." Throughout his political career, he had often taken positions at variance with what some considered liberal dogma. During the early fifties, he expressed concern over the dangers of internal subversion, criticized President Truman's China policy, and appeared to take little interest in the Supreme Court desegregation decision in 1954, declaring, "I never joined the Americans for Democratic Action or the American Veterans Committee. I'm not comfortable with those people." Hospitalized in December 1954 when the Senate censured Joseph R. McCarthy of Wisconsin, Kennedy did not reveal that he had intended to vote for censure until several years afterward. His hesitation over McCarthy was to a degree a family problem; his brother Robert served for a time as chief counsel for McCarthy's committee. Liberals charged that the Senator from Massachusetts, who had recently won a Pulitzer Prize for his book *Profiles in Courage,* showed more profile than courage. Unquestionably, Kennedy possessed a strong streak of conservatism; in addition, he disliked politicians who reacted as if with a conditioned response to an idea or a program simply because someone labeled it liberal or conservative.

Because it was essential to his plans, if he hoped to become the Democratic presidential nominee in 1960, but also from intellectual conviction, Kennedy moved steadily to the left after 1956. By the time of his candidacy (January 2, 1960), he had become certifiably liberal on the large issues of civil rights, civil liberties, and social justice. As President, his concern for such matters steadily deepened, and he became the first chief executive to express the moral obligation of the nation to the black. Backing his words with federal power in Alabama and Mississippi, he called upon the American people to recognize the plight of the black man as a moral issue "as old as the scriptures and . . . as clear as the American Constitution." The time had come for the nation to fulfill its commitment to the proposition "that race has no place in American life or law."

At the time he spoke these words, John Kennedy may not have been representative of the American Irish. Nonetheless, it was fitting that the first Irish-American President—a grandson of Boston ward leaders and nominated by the Irish bosses in the great Eastern and Midwestern cities—the ultimate success story of a formerly despised people, should be a man able to view compassionately the struggle of those in America who had not yet made it.

He died before he had really gotten his administration underway, and it will be hard for historians to evaluate him, so short a time was he given. We have some indications, however, that they will rate him higher than his contemporaries did. Although his place in history remains to be determined, within a year after his assassination Kennedy had gained a place in legend, one that grew with the murder of his brother, Robert, in the 1968 presidential campaign. The tragedy of the Kennedys was almost unbearable for their followers; Daniel P. Moynihan, Assistant Secretary of Labor, said after the President's death: "I don't think there's any point in being Irish if you don't know that the world is going to break your heart some day." John and Robert Kennedy were, in the words of James Reston, symbols of the tragedy and caprice of life. For the Kennedys the tragedy "was greater than the accomplishment, but in the end the tragedy enhances the accomplishment and revives the hope."

Sources

Burns, James M., *John F. Kennedy: A Political Profile,* New York, 1960.

Reston, James, "What Was Killed Was Not Only the President," *New York Times Magazine,* November 15, 1964.

Schlesinger, Arthur M., Jr., *A Thousand Days: John F. Kennedy in the White House,* Boston, 1965.

Sorensen, Theodore, *Kennedy,* New York, 1965.